Trinny and Susannah

What you wear can change your life

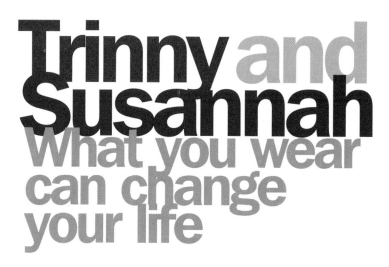

Trinny and Susannah

What you wear can change your life

**Trinny Woodall and
Susannah Constantine**

Photography by Robin Matthews

**Riverhead Books
New York**

To Zak, Joe, Esme, Cece and Lyla

The Berkley Publishing Group
Published by the Penguin Group
Penguin Group (USA) Inc.
375 Hudson Street, New York, New York 10014, USA
Penguin Group (Canada), 10 Alcorn Avenue, Toronto, Ontario M4V 3B2, Canada
(a division of Pearson Penguin Canada Inc.)
Penguin Books Ltd., 80 Strand, London WC2R ORL, England
Penguin Group Ireland, 25 St. Stephen's Green, Dublin 2, Ireland (a division of Penguin Books Ltd.)
Penguin Group (Australia), 250 Camberwell Road, Camberwell, Victoria 3124, Australia
(a division of Pearson Australia Group Pty. Ltd.)
Penguin Books India Pvt. Ltd., 11 Community Centre, Panchsheel Park, New Delhi—110 017, India
Penguin Group (NZ), cnr Airborne and Rosedale Roads, Albany, Auckland 1310, New Zealand
(a division of Pearson New Zealand Ltd.)
Penguin Books (South Africa) (Pty.) Ltd., 24 Sturdee Avenue, Rosebank, Johannesburg 2196,
South Africa

Penguin Books Ltd., Registered Offices: 80 Strand, London WC2R ORL, England

WHAT YOU WEAR CAN CHANGE YOUR LIFE

Text copyright © Susannah Constantine & Trinny Woodall 2004
Design and layout © Weidenfeld & Nicolson 2004
Photography by Robin Matthews
The BBC logo is a trademark of the British Broadcasting Corporation and is used under license.
BBC logo © BBC 1996
What Not to Wear logo © BBC 2002
Cover design by Lippa Pearce/Claire Vaccaro
Cover photo by Robin Matthews
Hair by Richard Ward Hair & Beauty, London
Makeup by Charlotte Ribeyro
Styling by Zoe Lem and Hayley Parsons
Research and coordination by Jessica Jones

PRINTING HISTORY
Previously published in hardcover in the UK by Weidenfeld & Nicolson, 2004, by arrangement with the BBC
First Riverhead trade paperback edition: February 2005
Riverhead trade paperback ISBN: 1-59448-148-2

This book has been catalogued with the Library of Congress.

PRINTED IN THE UNITED STATES OF AMERICA

10 9 8 7 6 5 4 3 2 1

CONTENTS

INTRODUCTION

We have no intention of writing our autobiographies so this book is the closest anyone will get to seeing inside the minds of Susannah and Trinny. You could call it our beauty biography, but this is so much more than a eulogy on particular face creams and mascara wands. We have gone into every aspect of looking good, from underwear to how to lay out your wardrobe. And we have thought about the concerns that worry women throughout their lives, at different stages of their lives.

We have witnessed time and again on our television program and in our clothing workshops how looking good can change a woman's life. In filming our most recent series for BBC1 we have learned more about women of different ages and lifestyles than ever before. We have lived the lives of mothers with toddlers and teenage daughters, women going through a midlife crisis, the loneliness of the woman looking for Mr. Commitment, and the scariness of menopause.

In doing this we have been able to incorporate our harvested knowledge into this book, and we would like to thank each and every contributor for allowing us to be them for the day. A large part of this book has sprung from these experiences because we have been able to understand how very confusing it can be for women moving on to other stages of their lives, how all-consuming the physical and emotional changes are that we have to go through during the course of our lives.

We have been able here to enlarge upon those areas that are the subject of our new series – the different stages of a woman's life, the times when change can bring about a loss of confidence and feelings of inadequacy. Looking good, and feeling that you are looking good, has an important psychological role to play in moving through the five life-changing stages of a woman's life.

The first is having a baby, and in our series, we went one

step further and looked at the lives of women who have more than one toddler under five.

Having children obviously changes the way you look at yourself. Your body has become functional and no longer an expression of a sexy wife or partner. Women at this point in life suddenly find themselves needing to wear clothes for practical rather than stylish reasons. "Is there any point in buying clothes when I don't know if I will ever be the same shape again?" is the resounding cry.

Having a baby changes a woman's body dramatically, making her feel less attractive. This in turn has a huge impact on her physical relationship with her partner, which encourages a vicious circle of negative feelings. She thinks it will never be possible to regain her old life when she looked and felt fantastic. Being a working mother adds to these feelings of guilt and exhaustion.

As to pampering, when are you ever going to get time for a facial or even a moment to buy and apply a new lipstick? You have spent nine months in a nursing bra. Can your boobs ever take anything underwired again? Your tummy has been reduced to semolina but you don't have the time to exercise or the energy to diet.

Then there is the financial side. You love your children to bits and you want to spend every last penny on them. This leaves little or nothing for you, which means having to prioritize on clothing and not making costly mistakes. The best way to combat the broke blues is to head for the No-cost wardrobe chapter.

Looking for Mr. Commitment is a common complaint at any age. Often the reason a woman is unable to find a perfect man is because she is putting them off with her lack of style.

This is a sad truth, but a very real one because the shallow male fraternity are initially attracted by how a woman looks. They don't give a damn whether she's a wonderful person inside. Their first thought is of sex and what a woman will look like without her clothes on.

For these women, more than for any other group in the new series, it was the packaging that was the most important thing to get right. Although we knew this and had to keep it in the back of our minds, we also had to think of the women's lifestyles because they couldn't be seen looking ready to drop their knickers in the school room or the courthouse.

Having said that, they had to be armed with enough appeal when walking down the aisle at the A&P to attract the ideal fella browsing through the lettuces.

Overridingly with this group the problem was a lack of self-esteem and feeling not good enough to be worthy of their prince. We really had to bolster our two final ladies' confidence with rousing encouragement, beautiful clothes and smoldering makeup. For one woman, in particular, makeup was anathema, something she felt she couldn't buy, let alone wear, because she felt so shitty about herself.

We hope our work will be their salvation from loneliness… Isn't it amazing what a bit of lip gloss and a well-turned leg can potentially do?

The women in a midlife crisis seemed to have either too much or too little on their plates. It was a question of being stuck in a rut and not being able to scramble out of it. Many of the women we met used the busy-ness of their lives as the excuse to have no time to deal with their appearance.

Common to all was a general sense of panic, the realization that maybe they had messed up their lives, of wanting to go back in time, not knowing how, realizing it was impossible, and being devastated by that fact. They wanted to change, but didn't know how.

A midlife crisis seemed to manifest itself in two ways, reflected in the two women we finally chose for the series.

One dressed far too young for her age, and the other had given in to frumpiness. Both suffered from a lack of identity.

Our first job was to make them look at themselves to see who they really were. This initially compounded the younger dresser's depression at not being young anymore. In the case of the frump, she had to rid herself of her dowdy self-image to realize that there was an attractive woman hiding inside.

It was wonderful to see them both emerge as independent women excited about their futures.

Glamorous teenage daughters do highlight the fact that a woman is aging and starting to lose her looks. It is natural that a certain amount of jealousy and competitiveness arises. It is, after all, the beginning of the next generation taking over.

If a woman has dedicated her life to being a mother, this is the point at which her role in life becomes confused. Her daughter is getting ready to leave the nest—what is her role? Is she no longer a mother? Does she go back to being an independent woman, or a wife? Has her relationship with her husband remained strong?

How does she feel about the fact that her daughter may now be more attractive to men than she is? Does she approve of this? Does she resent her daughter?

Alongside these doubts is the awareness of how much her body is changing. Clothes she used to consider sexy may now be out of date. Does she look like mutton dressed as lamb? She wonders if she's not turning into her own mother.

And she senses that her daughter is embarrassed about her, which makes her nervous about expressing herself as a woman rather than as a mother.

This woman now has to think about focusing more on herself, not easy when the last time she did this was many years ago. Most chapters in this book will help this woman.

Of the five stages we dealt with in making the new series, menopause was the one we knew least about. It was also the most depressing because so many women seem to give up once they reach menopause. They feel their life is over, that they have become invisible and are no longer making a mark in any shape or form on society.

We wanted to help give back the self-esteem of every single menopausal woman we came into contact with because we know the impact looking good can make on a woman's feelings of self-worth.

Here we learned about changing body shape, hot flashes, aches and pains and vaginal dryness.

And these are just the physical manifestations.

Emotionally, there is anxiety, depression, paranoia and lessening interest in sex to cope with.

What we hope we have shown in our series is that menopause is not the end of life as you know it; it is and can be the beginning of a new chapter, which once accepted, indeed embraced, can be a time of freedom and rediscovery.

Your children have probably flown from the nest, you may have paid off the mortgage, and for the first time in your life your world is truly your own. This, coupled with a spanking new look in hair, makeup and clothing, can be the most rewardingly unencumbered stage of all.

The two women we finally chose started out looking as though they were closer to being topped off by a gravestone than a shock of shiny new hair. They really did feel they had come to the end of the road. It was incredible to see their determination to rejuvenate themselves once shown how to dress and groom well. They both had the will to do this and because of that our job was made so much easier.

In this book we have gone into forensic detail on all the questions, complaints and anxieties women have shared with us. We couldn't have done this on our own because we don't share every beauty and clothing problem known to womankind; but we have learned. In order to help women we have had to come up with a solution for dilemmas that were once alien to us but are now all too familiar.

We have investigated practically every makeup and beauty product on the market and selected the ones we feel work best for a particular purpose. We have covered the problems, and in various categories listed products that are appropriate for different age groups.

We have religiously avoided the *People* and *US Weekly* spreads so it is here that you will see the two of us pregnant and pictured with our babies.

And speaking of pictures...we will show you how to look terrific in those holiday photographs – how to sit to best effect at a table or in a swimsuit, lounge attractively on a chaise, and look a whole lot better than who or what you are standing next to.

This book is not a retouched glossy magazine account of the road to perfection. It is the honest and truthful story of how to look at yourself and see what you can make better. We are not influenced by advertising (except when it comes to coffee!) so therefore the information is firsthand, tried and tested common sense.

Trinny
x

Susannah

01
Defin
your shape

While this is naturally the most fabulous book ever, indispensable and life changing, its information will have absolutely no effect unless you have appraised your shape. Oh God, what a vile and hideous thing to have to do. We are certain the idea of standing naked in front of a full-length mirror makes you want to reach for the nearest plastic bowl to vomit in. We are convinced you won't want to compound the horror by making your rear view available to criticism via a hand mirror reflecting the image of your butt in the bathroom looking-glass. For sure, an order from us to do it twice in one day (morning and night) will make you wonder whether we are writing from the goodness of our hearts or a sick desire to make you feel like shit. As we have always said, deciphering your flaws and assets is a crucial part of looking your best. If you won't do it, give this book to a friend who will and watch her blossom.

It took us a long time to realize the importance of body assessment. What we conveniently forgot was the fact that our bodies had changed over the years. Fad diets, pregnancy, exercise and lack of it had left us with bodies we no longer recognized. Because the changes happened slowly, we weren't aware that our figures were no longer lithe and lean, and consequently we were buying all the wrong clothes. To let you in on a secret, we only put ourselves under the microscope five or six years ago. Yes, we had a good knowledge of clothes, but this only became the "science" upon which we've built our careers after prodding and poking our parts with the precision of two neurosurgeons. And, girls, you absolutely HAVE to do this, however painful it might be.

Decoding your shape is not easy, especially as age-old misconceptions and insecurities get in the way. How do you know whether you have saddlebags, if you are an hourglass or a pear, or if your arms should be hidden at all times? It helps to do this with a good friend because the comparison will make you more aware of the way you are built. Introducing your eyes to your good points must be done in the morning before breakfast. We all feel thinner then, and more open to see what we like. The bad points become glaringly obvious at around 6 p.m., just as you are about to have a pre-dinner guzzle.

In both instances, take note of whether you are top- or bottom-heavy. Carrying the weight up top invariably means you have big boobs, fat arms, a wobbly tummy and a shorter neck, while your legs, butt and skin will be the envy of all your friends. Bottom bulk will often be topped by a long back, which means a flatter stomach because your intestines quite literally have more room. Your breasts will be smaller and your arms more shapely.

Talking legs, they, too, have variables and their shape and fat distribution will dictate what shoes and tights you wear. Same with a neck. If you think you look daft in a collar your neck is probably short. If thin chokers get lost, then your neck will be longer.

One time when a woman must reevaluate her shape is during menopause. The most common change is a thickening of the waist where the stomach takes over as a main body flaw and can become bigger than your chest size. You must learn to accept your figure at every stage of your life. Look to your mother as to how you will fare at menopause.

Only when you accept your body shape will you have the courage to move on. We sympathize and know this is an awful thing to ask of you, but please take our advice – it is the first step to a new you.

SUSANNAH

I can't believe I've ended up this shape. Although always curvaceous, the curves were where you'd expect them to be, like my waist. My boobs used to be an easy-to-handle C. My stomach lay within my body. My arms, while strong, never required total cover. Damn it, I used to be bloody perfect. I was in proportion. Not too fat, not too thin. Now, oh my God, now things are very different. A naked Susannah is like a fat white maggot, all folds and undulating movement. The breasts have engorged to an E cup, the stomach has emerged like a hernia, open and laid out for inspection above every waistband, and the arms, well, they are worryingly vast and soon to take over my entire body. This may sound exaggerated, but it's how I feel about the parts I don't like. Luckily for me, however, I have learned to block them out by appreciating what little there is left to love.

My arms
I never wear sleeveless tops because my upper arms are proportionately much chunkier than my wrists. My dainty forearms become a member of the same fat family when my whole arm is displayed. This is why I cover them totally or just show my wrists in three-quarter-length sleeves.

My tummy
To have this hanging over a too-tight waistband kills all the self-esteem I might need to get through the day. When I sit down, I always cover my belly with arms or a handy handbag. The best cover for my least favorite bit is a fitted top that hugs my boobs and flares out over the tummy.

My ankles
Aside from my wrists these are the only bits of my body I am happy to show naked. Because they are thin and shapely, I can wear all skirt lengths just so long as they don't reveal my terrible, wrinkly knees.

My neck
Weird thing to loathe, I know, but it's short and rather thick. It has no definition because it is topped by a jaw that dribbles down the gullet and makes me chinless but not a wonder. As if by magic, shirt collars erase all signs of my neck whereas round necks or turtlenecks make my face look as if I am being throttled.

My boobs
The key to these is to keep them covered but show them off. As they are so huge compared to other parts and because my skin is now getting wrinkly, it's important that the cleavage line is always covered by fitted tops that still define the shape of my boobs. A lack of cleavage line makes my boobs less in your face and more demure.

My bum
Love it. It's pert and high as a kite. I show it off at all times by wearing skirts and trousers that hug it lovingly. That way we can see that I have long legs.

I grew up skinny, and never really thought about my proportions until I was an adult. Even though I am 5'10" I didn't require extra-long leg length in trousers. My boobs have always been nonexistent and it has never concerned me, except when I am out shopping with Susannah and rather covet her ability to hold a deep-cleavage dress in place. It wasn't until I reached my thirties that I realized I didn't look that hot in dresses, and trousers looked best with a very high heel underneath to keep me in proportion, as I tend to carry my weight on my bottom half. When I follow the rules for what to wear for my shape, I get good wear out of an item. I make new discoveries every year about how to dress for my shape; my latest is to bulk up my top half to reduce the width of my bottom. But ultimately I have to balance out how I feel inside about my shape and how others see me. The truth is somewhere in between.

My arms
These are definitely an asset. They have always been toned (many years of driving a Fiat Panda without power steering) and I have never been shy of showing them off. As they are very long, I have to be careful never to wear mid-length sleeves, but most other shapes work fine.

My torso
I have a very long body, which causes problems when I am buying tops as they are all too short. Even though my stomach is good (goes with the long back) I feel it makes my legs appear even shorter so I tend to layer clothes on my top half. I will find a top longer and in a slightly darker shade to the one I want to wear and wear that underneath. This shortens my torso and by definition elongates my legs.

My boobs
I'm a flat-chested girl (normally flatter than this as I am still breastfeeding here) and there have been occasions when a chicken fillet filling was needed to give me some bulk on top.

My hips
Although skinny, I do have a bottom and thighs—saddlebags by another name. I don't look great in jeans-cut trousers in a thin fabric because they look too clingy. I am better off in trousers that are floaty or else cling over the bottom and go straight down from the widest part.

My legs
They are short, even though I am tall. I suffer from bad water retention so thick ankles are a permanent feature. My calves are chunky and my thighs are bulky. So I hate wearing skirts and dresses, and if I do wear either it will be over a pair of trousers so I can disguise where my bottom ends and my legs begin. In winter, boots are a godsend.

"I despise simplicity. It is the negation of all that is beautiful"

Norman Hartnell

You need to look at your body. Not every woman benefits from over-the-top dressing.

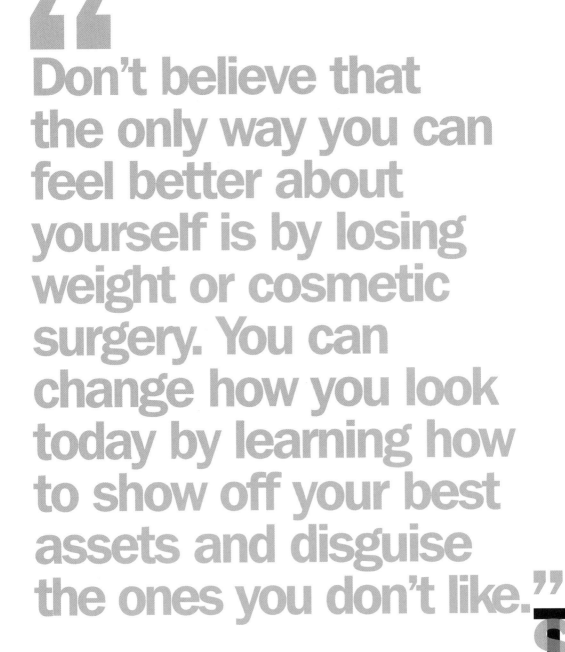

"Don't believe that the only way you can feel better about yourself is by losing weight or cosmetic surgery. You can change how you look today by learning how to show off your best assets and disguise the ones you don't like."

02

Under

In the same way that a stone foundation is the basis of a building, underwear is the source for creating a well-clad body. Not only do they make or break a look, good bras and panties can also radically change the shape of your body.

You may think it extreme that a humble pair of underwear can ruin an outfit. But think of Jennifer Lopez's butt, and the airtight clothes she encases it in. If her butt were kept cozy by a nice pair of comfortable knickers that didn't ride up her crack or leave room for a nasty draft between the waistline and her top, the smooth, rounded globes wouldn't be gouged by flesh-eating elastic.

Similarly, bras hold (quite literally) a girl's appearance in their cups. An astonishing 70 percent of us are wrecking our clothes with an ill-fitting brassiere. Just because it is worn underneath, its relevance, like underwear, is shunted down to the end of the style chain. It's tempting to think, "Who cares? No one is going to see it." Ah ha! Not so. These undergarments can often be spotted through fabric, and if they are not, then the impression badly fitting underwear makes on flab most definitely can.

A lady we dressed recently was a case in point. Partial to a friend's clothes, she accepted all things including her B-cup bras, into which she gleefully compressed her E-cup tits. The result was misshapen breasts that increased in number from two to four and looked fat instead of sexy.

Your underwear is particularly important if you are looking for Mr. Right. Most women think that underwear has to be either sexy or supporting – you *can* get underwear that is both. Likewise, if you are having a crisis of confidence, an easy way to feel desirable again is to invest in sexy and supportive bras and underwear. And for those women going through menopause, it helps to reupholster your body, rather like you would a tired old sofa!

If you are human and female you will have graying white

cotton, frayed elastic, skin-digging wire poking out from bras and stained gussets littering your underwear drawer. These cannot stay. All need dispersing to the big underwear graveyard in the sky. What you require, girls, is SUPPORT and SHAPING in all areas that have given in to gravity.

The older you get the more responsibilities you have, be it kids or mortgages. Money to burn on clothes becomes less. Surplus income should be spent on a sensible wardrobe that lasts. Well, what's the point if your tits are down by your ankles and your pock-marked arse bubbles the material of your trousers? If you want to feel good, you HAVE to fork out for excellent underwear. Your hard-earned cash is far better spent on bras, panties and reconstructive fortressing than a cute top from Marc Jacobs.

Underwear, like all fashion, can fall foul of trends. There was the time when women were encouraged to burn their bras. God forbid. Then Calvin Klein came in with the compromise T-shirt bra that did nothing other than obscure a nipple or two. During the late sixties and early seventies, underwear was pretty much discarded, a rebellion not only against the opposite sex but also against the constricting fifties that had us entombed in whalebone and elastic strong enough to mend a broken leg.

Nowadays, specialty panties, tights, all-in-ones and bras are industrially enhanced for the sole purpose of improving our shape in the same way corsets did in the nineteenth century. Underwiring, sucking in and winching may not be the sexiest impact upon disrobing, but it sure makes a woman feel good from the outside in.

We are passionate about the effects figure-forming underwear achieves because it gives instant gratification – it minimizes the hours required in the gym and maximizes the amount you can eat guilt-free.

Blow the diet and exercise regimen and invest in some great underwear.

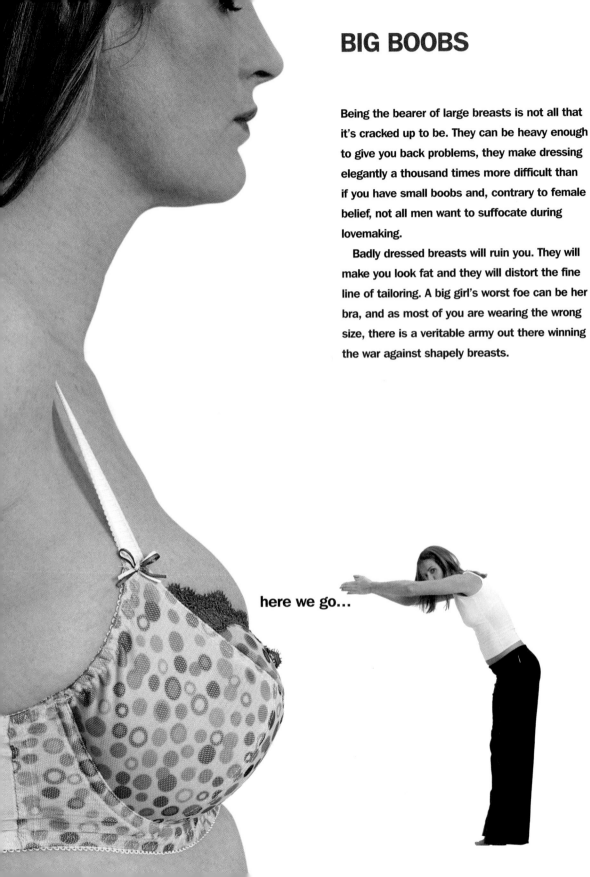

BIG BOOBS

Being the bearer of large breasts is not all that it's cracked up to be. They can be heavy enough to give you back problems, they make dressing elegantly a thousand times more difficult than if you have small boobs and, contrary to female belief, not all men want to suffocate during lovemaking.

Badly dressed breasts will ruin you. They will make you look fat and they will distort the fine line of tailoring. A big girl's worst foe can be her bra, and as most of you are wearing the wrong size, there is a veritable army out there winning the war against shapely breasts.

here we go...

Anyone with a D cup upward must realize
that a well-fitted bra is the most important item
in her wardrobe. Don't be scared of spending
three times as much as you would expect because
you will not regret it. If you can only afford
one bra, make sure it is made in a smooth
fabric. Avoid all lace and decoration
to broaden the bra's versatility.
Underwiring is essential as it will
push the boobs forward as well as
upward. The jutting action alone
will make you visibly lose pounds.

NO BOOBS

There is good flat-chested and bad flat-chested. If you have no tits but are blessed with an immaculate décolletage, like a virgin snow slope on a mountainside, all smooth and unmottled with no lines, you are one of the few flat-chested women who should wear deep V tops.

The rest of us, who don't have unblemished skin and probably suffer from sun damage from our teenage years, cannot. Expensive beauty products won't help either, although they can soften the skin. If you have this kind of skin you really need to ask yourself whether it's attractive enough to be on show or if you should cover up and enhance your shape through clever cosmetic molding.

But that doesn't mean resorting to a bra so padded that one does not even need to come up and take a pinch to see the fraud in your cleavage. There are alternatives. If you have a pigeon chest (where your breasts generally go in opposite directions leaving a raised crevass in the center), you need to fill the underneath

yeah, here they are

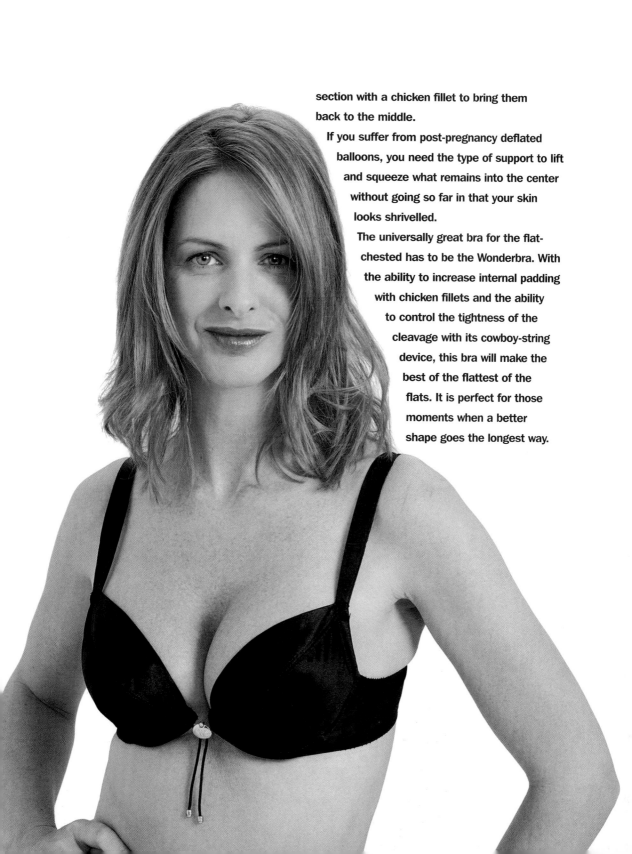

section with a chicken fillet to bring them back to the middle.

If you suffer from post-pregnancy deflated balloons, you need the type of support to lift and squeeze what remains into the center without going so far in that your skin looks shrivelled.

The universally great bra for the flat-chested has to be the Wonderbra. With the ability to increase internal padding with chicken fillets and the ability to control the tightness of the cleavage with its cowboy-string device, this bra will make the best of the flattest of the flats. It is perfect for those moments when a better shape goes the longest way.

SAGGY BOOBS

We find it amazing that so many women's boobs hang down to the top of their panty elastic... and that's *with* a bra. What's the point? Why bother wearing a bra at all if it can't combat the force of gravity? Sagging udders should be left to porky mammals slurping swill with 16 piglets attached to her teats. They don't do good bras for pigs but they do for us women.

A decent shape can do the same job as a cosmetic lift allowing you to wear and look great in clothes you haven't worn since the teen years.

The ultimate bra to hoist flagging breasts is the balcony. This design lovingly cups, ups and separates your breasts to provide perfect-shaped orbs.

yep, they're heading south

Susannah swears by it and won't even consider other varieties except when exercising or wearing a very flimsy T-shirt. The beauty of having one's tits elevated is the sudden appearance of a waist. Suddenly your boobs become boobs and not the extra tire around your middle. You look thinner, more shapely, and utterly wonderful.

FAT BACK

The bra is exquisite. Confectionery sweet and pretty as a picture. All embroidery and Belgian lace. Your boobs look fabulous from the front cradled in the cups. Good enough to eat, in fact. The shoulder straps are so delightfully fine you are happy to have them peek out from under your T-shirt. You assume the same about the back strap because that, too, is thread thin. The tragedy is, however, that those filament straps are acting like knives and slicing into any extra flesh you have about your back and shoulders. You might well love your boobs, but do you want another pair spilling over your bra strap on your back?

If you have a flabby back, and let's face it, most of us do, you need a wide strap that will distribute the pulling power over a wider area, thus reducing the flesh-digging capabilities.

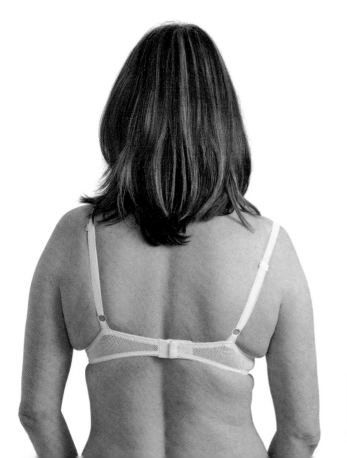

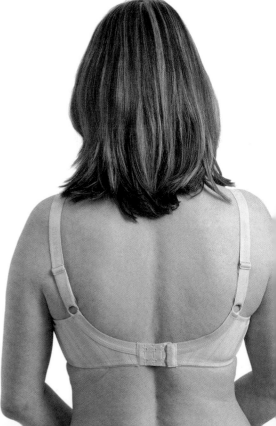

FLABBY TUMMY

As with any waistband laid upon a fat stomach, you
cannot have that of your underwear too tight. Like the bra
straps, it will dig in. Frumpy and sexless though it may
be, you need a waistband on your panties that reaches
up to your ribcage where there is less flab. The panties are
industrially reinforced by scientifically strengthened elastic.

"Brevity soul of

is the
lingerie
Dorothy Parker **"**

**The more upholstery
you have, the better.**

s

NO WAIST

So you thought the only way to create a waist was with the
help of a belt, high-waisted trousers or a corset. Winch
it in and the feminine curves arrive...well, maybe
with the corset, and perhaps with the other two,
but with these your body will be compromised
elsewhere. A constricting belt will make you
look like a knotted pair of stockings and a

tight waistband will flip the flab out from underneath to create a roll that rings the entire waist. Not the right look when aspiring to an hourglass shape. The corset is very effective but hopeless when worn under a smooth, tight fabric; every whalebone will be seen.

The desired effect is one that looks seamless and the only way to achieve this is with an all-in-one body. Be sure it's made in a smooth, nylon-esque fabric so that whatever is worn on top skims off it. Anything that sticks will give the game away.

SAGGY ARSE

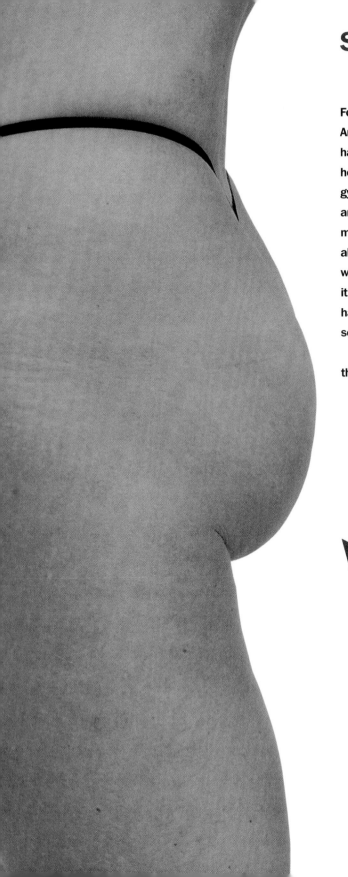

For a lucky few this is not an issue.
Any woman who is a pear shape will definitely
have a saggy arse (unless she is a very good
horse rider or obsessive about lunging in the
gym). In fact, for most of us there is a certain
amount of sag going on. Think of that awful
moment in the fitting room with the mirrors that
allow you to see your backside: half of you
wants to see that view; the other half wishes
it wasn't there. What you don't see, you don't
have to address. Bullshit. How many people
see your behind before they see you?

The g-string is the Number One enemy of
the saggy arse. Offering absolutely no support,

it enhances and encourages gravity to pull down those butt cheeks even farther. The only time to wear a g-string is under a pair of trousers with a thick fabric that in itself offers a bit of a butt lift.

The ultimate solution is a pair of contouring knickers that have built-in lift. Although seduction is then out of the question, the silhouette on offer in a pair of these will give a new lease on life to dresses and skirts once banished to the back of the wardrobe. There is always the opportunity to slip them off in the bathroom and come out pantyless (a slightly better turn-on) should that moment of seduction arrive.

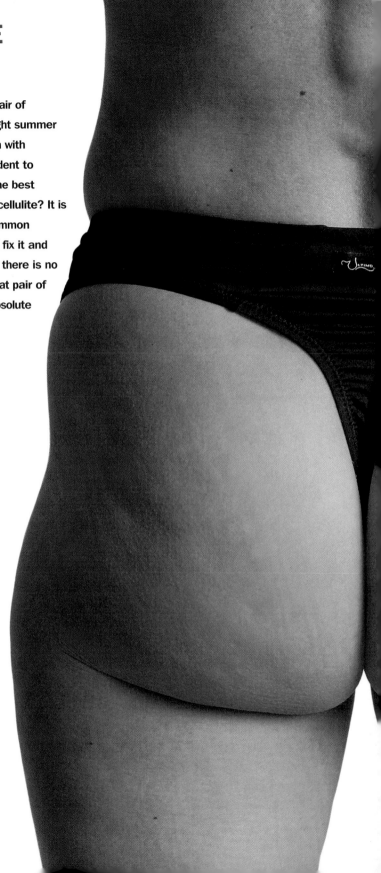

CELLULITE ARSE

How many of us have picked up a pair of gorgeous white trousers or a fab tight summer skirt, taken them to the fitting room with anticipation and felt utterly despondent to discover that, once on, they were the best advertisement for your burgeoning cellulite? It is such a depressing yet incredibly common problem. There are creams that will fix it and diets that will help it, but ultimately there is no better camouflage than a really great pair of latex bum-and-thigh panties. Our absolute favorites are Spanx Power Panties.

aaagh!

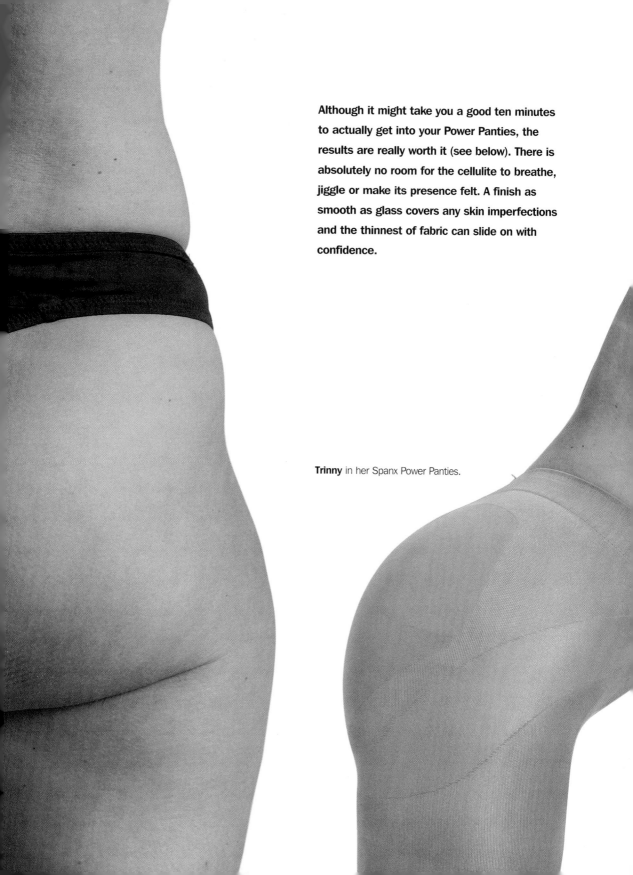

Although it might take you a good ten minutes to actually get into your Power Panties, the results are really worth it (see below). There is absolutely no room for the cellulite to breathe, jiggle or make its presence felt. A finish as smooth as glass covers any skin imperfections and the thinnest of fabric can slide on with confidence.

Trinny in her Spanx Power Panties.

BIG THIGHS AND SADDLEBAGS

Most pear-shaped women suffer from big thighs and saddlebags, and most pear-shaped women also possess far too many bikini briefs (bought in packs of three) in their underwear drawer, some with extra-tight white piping that grabs hold of their flesh and further enhances what they most wish to hide. Encased in a pair of too-tight trousers (with no pockets to disguise the area) the entire display reveals bodily defects in all their glory, leaving little to the imagination. Only supermodels look good in bikini briefs.

whoa

The rest of us need to take stock of our underwear drawer and really ask ourselves if what's there is doing anything for our body. Even if you are a lingerie aficionado, the satin and lace cami-panties will do nothing for your big thighs and saddlebags. **THROW THEM OUT NOW**, and go and invest in a bum-and-thigh panty with extra-thick lycra (see right) that will redistribute the flesh around the bum and thigh area and give you the appearance that you are thinner than you actually are.

According to a leading bra manufacturer, 70 percent of women wear the wrong-sized bra. Unless you get the underwear right, all your clothes will look bad. We have never met a woman with the perfect underwear in her closet. Check yours now. It is time and money well spent. 𝓽𝓼

03

Colo

People who understand color look more interesting, more in control, more confident, more self-assured, and more attractive. Color has the power to make you look healthy or unhealthy, thin or fat, short or tall. Wearing the wrong color scheme for you could make you look like a long-term heroin abuser rather than the balanced-diet yoga queen you long to be.

And entombing your giant arse in black won't make it disappear. You'll only look slimmer if you're wearing all black. You may think this is rich coming from us, two women who avoid the funereal color at all costs, but in this instance, it really does work...unless it doesn't suit you. Black is not the only color that can achieve this. Any color worn head to toe will have the same effect, as long as it's a color that suits you.

Got up this morning feeling like shit? Don't reach for the vodka bottle, the cure lies in your wardrobe. It's amazing how wearing one of the right colors for you can change your mood from deepest, darkest gloom and doom to annoyingly chirpy and effervescent.

While you need confidence to wear color, wearing the right color will give you that confidence. Why fit in to a situation, be it at a party or at work, when you can stand out as an individual? Believe it or not, there was a time when our appearance trailed behind our personalities. Susannah had a fondness for black and white and Trinny was a smudge of mismatched pastel, which later looked like something that the cat had thrown up.

It didn't start to come together for us until we began emulating Mother Nature's palette. Instead of thinking boiled sweets, we began looking at the sunset, an autumn tree, the fire, and hey, presto, things began to work. The trouble was, Susannah didn't look great in her tree colors and Trinny looked dire in the colors of the dawn. We hadn't worked out our own color groupings.

Having now dressed thousands of women, we have figured out how to do this. Consider yourself lucky that we've made all the mistakes in order to prevent you from doing the same.

The choice of color in clothing is immense and therefore utterly confusing. How the hell do you work out whether buttercup yellow is your thing or if eggplant should be on your butt rather than your plate? It's actually very easy, and the answer will again be in your wardrobe.

Take, for example, your favorite color. Is it blue, red, pink, green? As we all know, there isn't just one shade of blue, red, pink or green. If it's your favorite color you will definitely have different shades of it in your wardrobe. So let's say it's blue. You've probably got a navy, a pale icy blue, a bright blue and a sea-green blue. If Trinny were to do this test, the navy blue would wash out her complexion and give her darker circles under her eyes than she already has, and the bright blue would wear her. The pale blue would be too cold and wash her out as much as the navy, but the sea-green blue does everything to enhance her features. Her eyes look bluer, her skin looks clearer and her hair looks richer.

We've had many sleepless nights worrying over this, but after hours of brain-teasing we have honed the dilemma of color into two sections – how to pick the colors that suit you and what to wear with them. Follow these suggestions and you'll kiss color disasters goodbye.

And remember, even if your hair goes gray or you decide to change its color in a mad, midlife crisis moment, your color palette will always stay the same.

Menopausal women tend to stop wearing colors and shroud themselves in disappearing shades. Women with toddlers take to baby pink and baby blue. Women whose daughters have suddenly turned into beautiful young women shouldn't try to emulate their style of clothing, but they can compete on color. This could be your chance to educate your daughter on how to wear color.

HOW TO WORK OUT WHICH COLORS SUIT YOU

Go into your wardrobe and pick out the clothes in the colors you wear most often. Don't choose on the basis of whether that item of clothing actually suits your shape or if it cost you an arm or leg. This is about how the precise shade of a color works with your face.

Take the pile to a full-length mirror in good daylight and sort by color. Make a pile of blues, reds and so on. Taking one category at a time, put each item up against your face – and see what it does. Do your eyes look brighter? Your dark circles worse? Does your skin look radiant or does it go totally flat? You will soon know which shades of which colors are best for you.

Once you have your final pile of shades that suit you best, go to our color charts to find out which section (Cool and Bright, Warm, or Mid-Tones) you belong to. We are not looking for a perfect match here, but you should have at least four of the colors from one of the sections in your pile.

Left Trinny in navy; a bad choice because it does nothing for her complexion and highlights the black circles under her eyes, even though she has had a good night's sleep.
Right Sea-green blue is one of Trinny's best colors. It lifts her complexion, brightens her eyes and complements her hair.

HOW TO WORK OUT WHICH COLORS SUIT YOU

Once you have established which color category you are in, you might find that the green that is suggested is not the one you have worn before – but it will suit you more than the green in your pile.

When you have worked out your final colors, move on to our color coordination pages to see our suggestions for ways to wear each individual color (see pages 60–93).

We have taken 16 basic colors (including black and white) and shown what colors to wear with them. In all instances, the color on the left is the basic dominant color, the two colors next to it are ideal coordinates, and the color on the right is an accent color. This will look great as an accessory or in a scarf or detail, or as a secondary color to wear when you are feeling extra-confident.

Left This is one of Susannah's worst colors. It completely flattens her complexion and deadens the shine in her hair.
Right Watermelon is one of her best colors, bringing alive her skin, eyes and hair.

COOL AND BRIGHT

People suited to cool colors generally have the following characteristics: When their hair goes gray it does so beautifully as a true salt-and-pepper, with no hint of ginger or yellow. They definitely do not have auburn hair, hazel eyes and freckly skin. Their skin is most likely to be alabaster white or olive. Their eyes have a dark rim around the iris or may be a very dark to mid brown. People in this color spectrum look truly terrible in any type of brown; rust, dull apricot and beige are nearly as bad.

Black, on the other hand, is a good color on you and can be worn right up to your neck;

it doesn't drain your face, like it does to people who suit warm or mid-tone colors. Navy works too, but to wear it in a youthful way, make sure you team it with turquoise or emerald greens.

You look great in very strong purples. Gray is one of your main colors; don't think you have to be old and fuddy duddy to wear it – it will look chic rather than aging. If your hair has already lost its youthful color and is on the way to being white, gray is one of your best colors.

Icy-pale colors work too, but make sure they are not teamed with black as it will take all the subtlety out of them.

You most suit

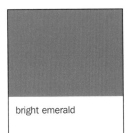

bright emerald

bright turquoise

navy

dark gray

You least suit

beige

tobacco

apricot

dark coffee

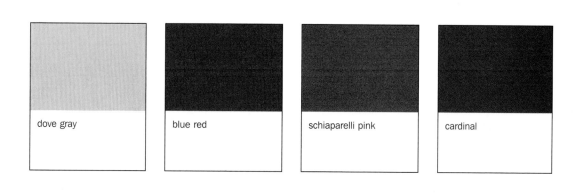

dove gray

blue red

schiaparelli pink

cardinal

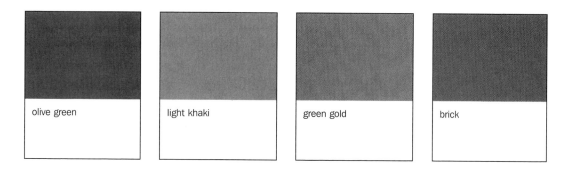

olive green

light khaki

green gold

brick

WARM

People who fall into this category are easy to spot. The majority have some red in their hair, from rich brown through to auburn or ginger – there may even be some strawberry blondes.

When women in this category go gray, they are desperate to have their hair colored because it can take on an unattractive hue. Their eyes might be blue, but not that bright turquoise blue; eye color is more likely to be brown, hazel or a duller green. Their skin tone might be a little sallow or freckly, but generally not dark or mid-brown.

This color grouping looks truly appalling in black; it is their worst color by far. Navy comes in a close second, followed by any shade of pink or pastel blue. They generally do not suit colors that are cold or have too much blue in them, like a hot pink or bright turquoise. Gray is not great either, as it will totally wash out their complexion.

The best colors are autumnal – think of a New England landscape. Rusts, khakis, warm rich browns, olive greens and tomato reds. Some can wear blue if it's more of a teal blue. Others

You most suit

tomato red

olive

dark tobacco

sea green

You least suit

pale rose pink

hot pink

beige

icy blue

can get away with brick, as long as it's not too pink. You could still be a Warm and not suit apricot.

If you don't suit olive and mustard, you don't belong in the Warm section at all.

It is important to remember that Warm is the easiest category to know for sure that it's right, far more so than Cool and Bright or Mid-Tones. Some people cross categories, but if you suit Warm you will definitely not be in doubt.

mustard

brown burgundy

light cream

pink burgundy

sky blue

dark gray

navy

black

MID-TONES

If you suit Mid-Tones you veer toward muted bright colors. Too bright and they overwhelm you; too pastel and they take the color out of your complexion. Your skin might have blue undertones and without makeup you can appear quite washed out. At the other end of the scale, you might have a peaches-and-cream complexion. Your eyes are predominantly green, aqua or blue.

You look great in purples, especially wisteria and lavender. Soft blues work well, too. You can sometimes get away with navy, but your best blue is probably periwinkle. Burgundy works well, from plums to more pinkish hues. Warm pastels, like powder pink or blue, are also good.

When you are looking at your wardrobe, discard all very cold bright colors, like blue red and cardinal purple, and all colors that are really

You most suit

clear red

hot pink

dark lavender

lemon yellow

You least suit

rust

green gold

salmon

warm beige

dirty, like beige or khaki. Your green is a sage (like the fresh, newborn leaf of an olive tree as opposed to its dying neighbor). If you are choosing purple, avoid that bright, cold tone and go for a dark lavender instead.

You will tend to wear similar tones of coordinating colors. If you get the color mix right, they will make you look more alive and you will begin to see a difference. People will start to comment on how well you look and notice the color of your eyes for the first time. But, most importantly, your wardrobe will be free of those annoying items that don't go with anything else. You will save money, you'll look great and you will no longer have to agonize over what to wear.

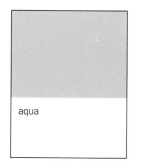

aqua

sage

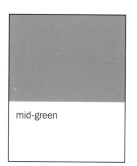

mid-green

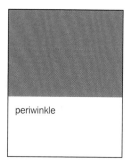

periwinkle

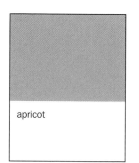

apricot

icy blue

charcoal

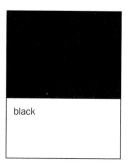

black

BEIGE

Boring beige! No more. You don't have to wear beige as though you're office furniture. How about breathtaking, beautiful beige? This is one of the most versatile of colors.

Whatever your skin tone, you will find a beige to suit you and whatever the occasion, you can rise to it in a well-put-together beige outfit. It's a sophisticated alternative to white in the summer and much more slimming.

For the evening, a chic, soft beige outfit will have you wafting through all the boring blacks like a celestial being. You'll make sure you're noticed without screaming "Look at me" or dancing on the tables.

If you're one of those who can't wear gray, then beige is definitely for you and, yes, you *can* wear it to work, but please not head to toe or you might easily be mistaken for the filing cabinet.

Don't kill your beautiful beiges with dark brown leather shoes and handbags. Soft suede or velvet accessories are ideal.

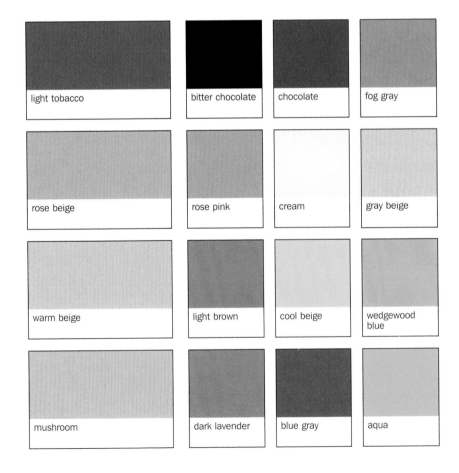

light tobacco	bitter chocolate	chocolate	fog gray
rose beige	rose pink	cream	gray beige
warm beige	light brown	cool beige	wedgewood blue
mushroom	dark lavender	blue gray	aqua

“I find that this color works best for me during the winter when my skin is at its palest. If worn with a tan it can look quite tacky. ”

GRAY

Gray is not a color everyone can wear. If you have red hair, hazel eyes and freckly skin it is not the color for you in any shape or form. If you have deep blue eyes and black hair, or your hair is turning the type of gray you don't have to dye, then nearly any shade of gray is one of your best colors. If you are desperate to keep your hair dyed you will find gray suits you less.

A lot of people don't like gray because it was the color of their school uniform, but it can be one of the most sophisticated colors to wear if you know how.

Gray is mostly a daytime color, except when it's a beautiful silvery satin. It is a good alternative to black.

When wearing gray, remember that the second strongest color in your outfit should be tonal, not too contrasting. Brighter colors can be added in smaller amounts.

A lot of people ruin gray with black accessories. Contrasting colors look best – for day, choose chocolate-brown shoes or boots (suede is better than leather) and at night, high-heeled shocking pink or red pumps.

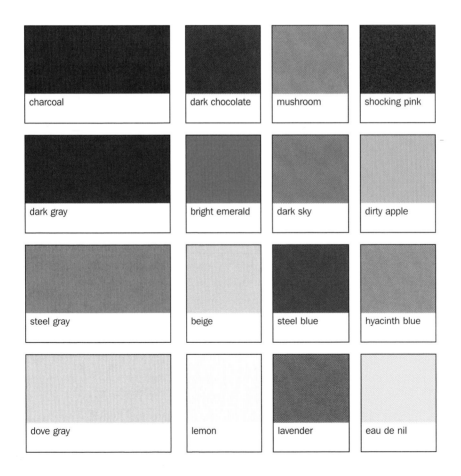

charcoal

dark chocolate

mushroom

shocking pink

dark gray

bright emerald

dark sky

dirty apple

steel gray

beige

steel blue

hyacinth blue

dove gray

lemon

lavender

eau de nil

" This color gray is quite dark for me to wear if I just wore it with white. I need the warmth of the blue to carry it off. My accessories are in similar tones of dark green or turquoise. **"**

YELLOW

So many people shy away from yellow because it scares them. Who would want to look like a giant custard? But yellow is also the color of the sun so, when worn correctly, it can have you stepping down the street in a blaze of glory. In general, avoid yellow if you have sallow skin – it will make you look like a jaundice victim – but if you're black or brown skinned, tanned or even ivory, then take the plunge.

Yellow is all about how you coordinate it. Strong gold and buttercup yellows love hot company, such as burnt orange, tobacco and a flash of bright red. If pale yellow is your color, go for a more demure look and team it with pale aqua and ivory, or soft orange and pale rose to create a shimmery-soft sorbet effect.

If you're still afraid, start out by wearing yellow in soft-textured fabrics like chiffon or viscose knits. These will break up the surface and be a little less attention-grabbing. But if you are happy to bathe in the spotlight, yellow is for you.

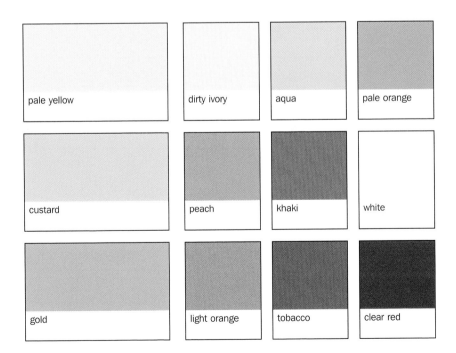

pale yellow | dirty ivory | aqua | pale orange

custard | peach | khaki | white

gold | light orange | tobacco | clear red

❝ I wear this color when I'm at my happiest. I never seem to be attracted to it when I'm feeling low. Maybe I should because it improves my mood so much. ❞

LIGHT BLUE

What's not to love about light blue? Everyone can wear it, and if you have blue eyes it's a perfect color for you. The problem is that because light blue is so easy we often don't think – just sling it on with everything and get it totally wrong. Take a look. Is the light blue you're wearing the right blue for you?

When you're putting your blues together, think of the colors of the sea, from the warm tones of a tropical lagoon to the icy shades of a glacier, and you won't go far wrong. Many women tend to think of light blue as a sporty color and wear it exclusively with jeans or sweats. Well, that's okay, but why not consider an aqua evening dress? Or a powder-blue suit teamed with french navy and a touch of vivid sea green?

A lot of pale blues look great with white – clean and fresh. Contrary to popular belief, they are not good with black.

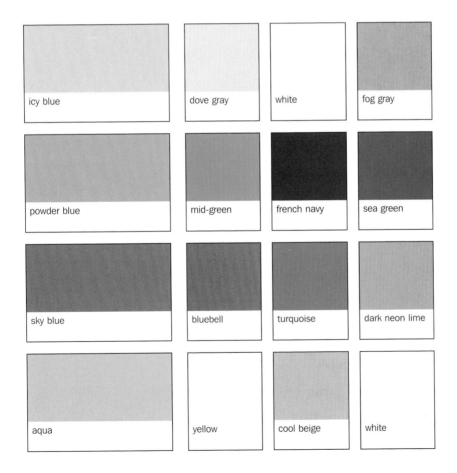

icy blue	dove gray	white	fog gray
powder blue	mid-green	french navy	sea green
sky blue	bluebell	turquoise	dark neon lime
aqua	yellow	cool beige	white

"If I were to wear a T-shirt in plain pale blue, it would look terrible. The way for me to wear this color is either to have it in a pattern with other complementary colors, like this shirt, or to wear it in a fabric with a bit of shine."

DARK BLUE

You might have an aversion to dark blue because it makes you feel like you've just joined the forces or been promoted to head nurse. You might even be a head nurse, but that doesn't mean you have to wear dark blue as though it's a uniform.

There are many different shades of dark blue and once you have found your shade you will wear it again and again.

In general, dark blues work well with other darker colors. Susannah, for instance, finds that wearing a brighter royal blue and a deep burgundy lifts and intensifies her french navy clothing, while a pale beige provides a sophisticated contrast.

Trinny cannot wear french navy at all, but she looks sumptuous in slate blue.

At all costs, avoid the cliché of dark blue with white – unless you're actually planning to weigh anchor and set sail.

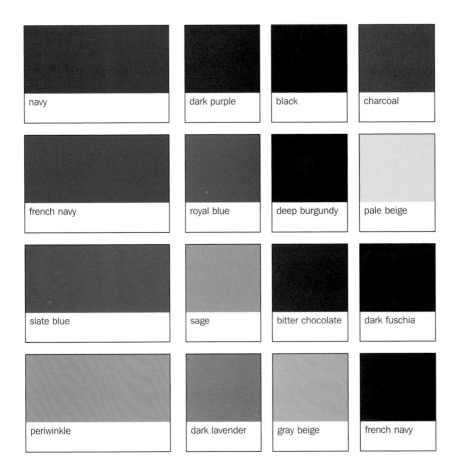

navy   dark purple   black   charcoal

french navy   royal blue   deep burgundy   pale beige

slate blue   sage   bitter chocolate   dark fuschia

periwinkle   dark lavender   gray beige   french navy

❝ I love this combination because it's so rich. These are the colors I wear if I feel myself veering toward black. **❞**

DARK GREEN

"Blue and green should never be seen"…Oh really? We say: "Green loves blue like I love you." Take a look at the infinite variety of landscapes where dark greens blend with blues and browns and flashes of brighter colors. Check out a peacock's tail.

Dark green is another color that many of us avoid for fear of getting it wrong, and indeed it does require courage to make these seemingly unusual color combinations – racing green with sea green, dark purple and mustard – look good. We promise you that they do work and if you dare to wear dark green in all its glory you will feel quite special and different in a world of navy and black.

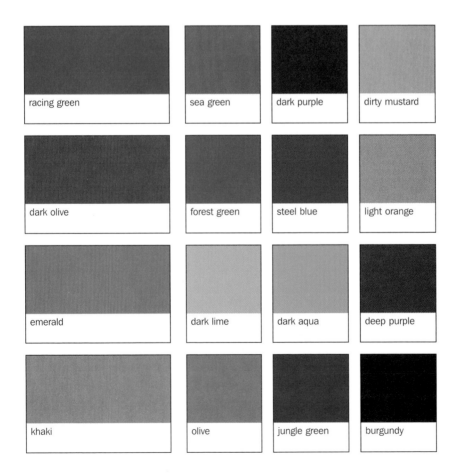

racing green	sea green	dark purple	dirty mustard
dark olive	forest green	steel blue	light orange
emerald	dark lime	dark aqua	deep purple
khaki	olive	jungle green	burgundy

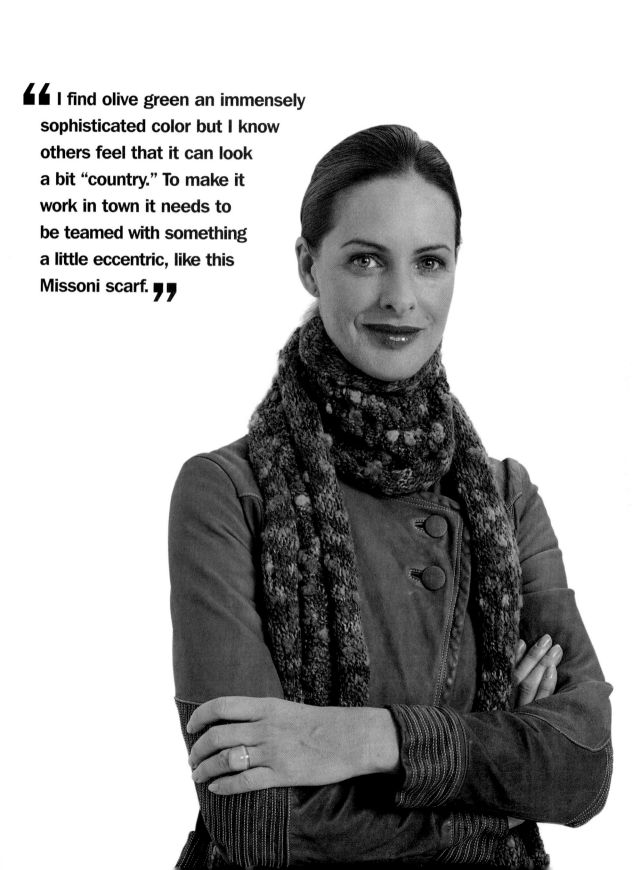

"I find olive green an immensely sophisticated color but I know others feel that it can look a bit "country." To make it work in town it needs to be teamed with something a little eccentric, like this Missoni scarf."

PALE GREEN

For summer, pale green is ideal. It works really well with other greens, but the trick is to wear just enough green but not so much that you look like one of Robin Hood's Merry Men. And avoid wearing brown with pale green or you risk going one step further and resembling one of the trees in Sherwood Forest.

Turquoise, yellow, deep purple or even shocking pink can be great with some greens and will make sure you stand out in the forest.

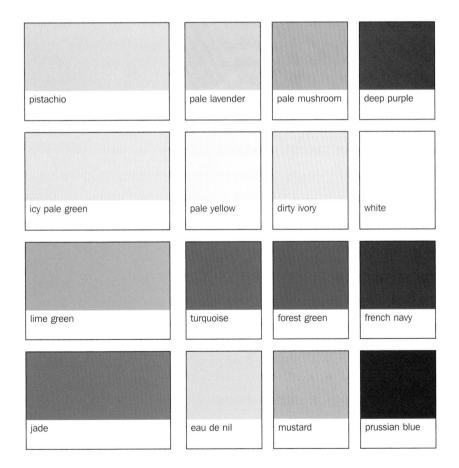

pistachio	pale lavender	pale mushroom	deep purple
icy pale green	pale yellow	dirty ivory	white
lime green	turquoise	forest green	french navy
jade	eau de nil	mustard	prussian blue

" The only way I can wear a color this bright is to combine it with a darker color, like this navy skirt, but it still needs something extra. The rose gives a focal point that balances the stronger colors. **"**

TURQUOISE

The fastest way to kill turquoise is to wear it with black. Yet so many of us do exactly that. This wonderful color really comes into its own in the warm months. Trinny and Susannah have loads of it in their summer wardrobes.

During the summer, turquoise looks fabulous with beige and white and with pale greens.

Although turquoise is harder to wear in the darker days, don't overlook it as a means of enriching your winter wardrobe. Team it with navy, deep fuschia and vivid greens to create a glamorous jewel-like effect.

sea green

bright green

emerald

aqua

turquoise

aqua green

lime

french navy

deep aqua

dirty pink

deep fuschia

apple green

" I suit a very deep turquoise, nearly green, which doesn't actually work with white. It looks its best when teamed with darker, stronger colors. "

PURPLE

From the palest lilac to the deepest plum, find the purple that's yours and then work it in throughout your wardrobe. Do try to avoid dressing entirely in purple, though. This is strictly the preserve of bishops.

Purple makes an excellent base color because it's easy to match and works in so many ways. Wear it sedately with olives, burgundies and deep green, or add pizzazz with fuschia, strong pinks and even orange. The wearing of purple was once restricted exclusively to royalty and it's still a symbol of all that's luxurious.

Purple is a really good alternative for those who can't wear burgundy, and it's just so much more regal than navy blue.

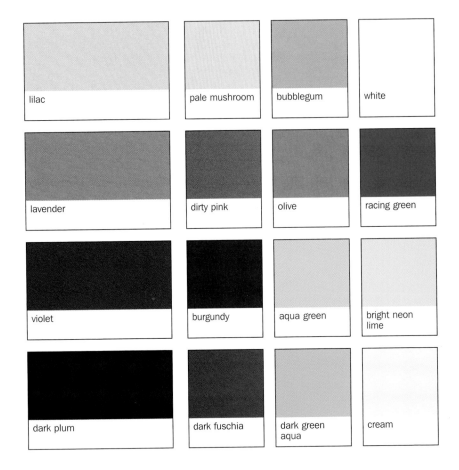

lilac	pale mushroom	bubblegum	white
lavender	dirty pink	olive	racing green
violet	burgundy	aqua green	bright neon lime
dark plum	dark fuschia	dark green aqua	cream

❝ Colors that are too dark tend to wash out my face so I've chosen my best green to lift the purple and lend an added richness to the velvet. **❞**

"when in

wear re

not if it doesn't suit you. 5

doubt
d...."

Bill Blass

RED

"I can't wear red." Well, you may be right. Red is difficult to wear and you really must find the right tone for your complexion. If you have even a touch of ruddiness in your skin, if you are just slightly sunburned or a fake-tan devotee, red will only bring out the lobster in you.

Surprisingly, red can look its very best against pale white skin or black skin, as well as with the beige skin tones.

The trick with red is to keep it hot. Wear it with pink and orange and tobacco and fuschia. There's no point trying to tone down red. Pump it up. Wear it full-blast or don't wear it at all.

The most common mistake is to team red with black or white, or both. Don't do it.

tomato

tobacco

brick

dusty pink

raspberry

hot pink

fuschia

violet

blue red

shocking pink

bright orange

plum

"This is the only red that I have in my wardrobe. Solid red just wears me but broken up into this pattern, with the pink tones further brought out by the necklace, I can just about get away with it."

BURGUNDY

If burgundy is your color, like it is mine, then you have hit the jackpot in making color coordination easy. Burgundy is endlessly versatile. I love it with all shades of pink and flame-inspired oranges and reds.

It breaks my heart when I see this rich color deadened by navy blue or black. It is, however, a great alternative to black because it is dark and makes you feel slim.

Burgundy can be a very aging color if it is too dull and cold a shade, or if you have warm-toned skin and hair. It particularly suits olive skin.

Do not wear black accessories with your beautiful burgundy outfit. If you don't have a pair of burgundy, fuschia pink or rust-colored shoes in your wardrobe, go for chocolate brown or olive green.

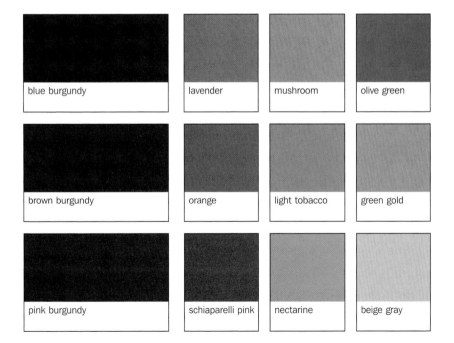

blue burgundy	lavender	mushroom	olive green
brown burgundy	orange	light tobacco	green gold
pink burgundy	schiaparelli pink	nectarine	beige gray

"When I wear this outfit I feel good. It can make a tired face look a bit chirpier because these colors bring out my features the best. I can be pale or tanned and it will still look good. Missoni is one of the best designers when it comes to understanding how to put colors together."

ORANGE

Orange is much more forgiving than red, but it can still be difficult on pinkish skin tones. If you are of a rosy complexion, choose your orange with care, but if you have a suntan or you are olive or dark skinned, go for it.

In summer you can be a riot of glorious orange light, like Van Gogh's sunflowers, and in winter you can be as warm as a log fire blazing in a brick hearth. These are the tones to look for (not those from a fizzy drink).

Almost every shade of orange has its complementing shade of pink; they were pretty much born for each other.

Orange, rust and tobacco are good colors for accessories to wear with orange and they are a livelier alternative to brown.

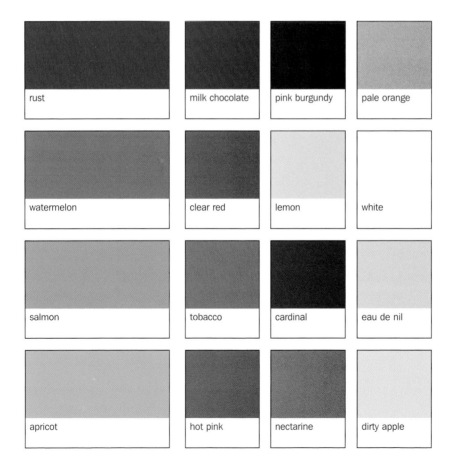

rust	milk chocolate	pink burgundy	pale orange
watermelon	clear red	lemon	white
salmon	tobacco	cardinal	eau de nil
apricot	hot pink	nectarine	dirty apple

" I can never wear orange around my face but I'm always drawn to it as a very happy color. It looks great with this burgundy, which is one of my favorite colors. **"**

PINK

When you were a little girl, did you go overboard on pink?

And have you now banished it from your life forever and replaced it with the dark forces of purple and black? But if your wardrobe is still overflowing with pink, we can bet that you are wearing lots of shades that don't suit you.

First, get out each garment and do the color test. Do you see a breathtaking vision or just a *blancmange*? Not sure? Ask your ruthless friend. Then look at our color charts to find colors to enhance and coordinate with your shade of pink – apart from pink.

If, on the other hand, you are an undercover goth who wouldn't be seen in your coffin wearing pink, then we feel that you are really missing out. Pink can be hot and sexy, and the softer shades are very appealing to the eye.

rose quartz

icy blue

pistachio

pale taupe

nectarine

pale brick

dull apricot

mushroom

bubblegum

purple

orange

forest green

schiaparelli pink

dark orange

light orange

dark eau de nil

Deep pink is a color I wear far more in the summer; the winter sees me running back toward burgundy.

BROWN

As with gray, a lot of women won't wear brown because it was the color of their school uniform. If you are not wearing brown you're really missing out because there is a beautiful brown for nearly everyone.

When you think of brown, don't think "detention," think cappuccino, chocolate, camel, sand, biscuit, tan, tobacco, mink, terracotta, puce, mahogany and…sable.

The only women who have difficulty wearing brown are those who suit very cool colors, generally those with pale, pale skin and dark blue eyes or the darkest tones of skin.

Most browns will look elegantly understated worn with the right tone of gray, while dark browns always look stylish with black. Warmer browns are great with green gold and also rust.

Brown is also a really useful color for accessories. Brown leather, in particular, looks richer and more expensive than black and is far more versatile in working with the other colors in your wardrobe.

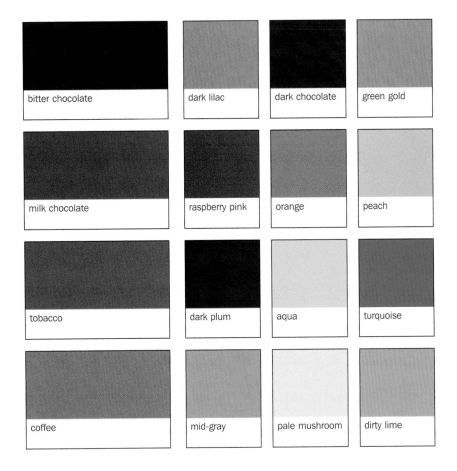

bitter chocolate	dark lilac	dark chocolate	green gold
milk chocolate	raspberry pink	orange	peach
tobacco	dark plum	aqua	turquoise
coffee	mid-gray	pale mushroom	dirty lime

> **Dark brown on its own, especially in wool, washes me out. The solution is to wear it in a luxurious fabric like velvet, which gives an added richness, making it wearable for me.**

WHITE

Mistake number 1: almost everyone thinks that white is just one color.

Mistake number 2: almost everyone buys every shade of white and thinks it will suit them because "it's just white."

White can be sharp and bright or it can be warm and creamy, like ecru. You have to find the shade that is right for you.

If bright white suits you, it will have a wonderfully uplifting effect on a tired day, lighting up your eyes and giving a natural reflection to your face. But if it is not your color, it will totally wash you out.

Once you have found your white, go out and buy several fitted white T-shirts in that shade (taking care that they are the right cut for your body shape). This is every woman's essential item for dressing down a smart skirt, wearing with jeans, under blouses and tank tops, and with sweats.

A word of warning: chunky white cotton knits only look good on Ralph Lauren models.

A second word of warning: in our opinion, the biggest fashion crime is the round-necked, loose-fitting, half-sleeved, white polyester blouse. If you own one of these, burn it.

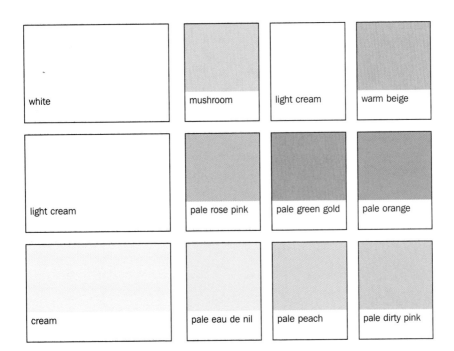

white · mushroom · light cream · warm beige

light cream · pale rose pink · pale green gold · pale orange

cream · pale eau de nil · pale peach · pale dirty pink

Bright white, apart from reminding me of my school shirt, is a color that really drains me, yet ecru (a much warmer white) can really lift me and make my skin glow. It's amazing how such a small variation in color makes such a big difference in how I look.

BLACK

Black is not a color. It is an absence of color. It is a drama, a pool of nothingness, a depth.

Do not treat black lightly. It is not a background for bright colors, nor is it a catch-all shade for shoes, handbags and dreary suits.

Black goes with black, and that's that. Okay, you may team it with brown for chic winter daywear, or with flashes of gunmetal or dove gray for special evenings, but those are our only concessions.

Black is the most abused and misused color (or non-color) of them all. It should be reserved for special occasions and funerals; instead, it is worn in offices, shops, bars and restaurants the length of this land. Black has become the tedious uniform of modern women. We now call upon you to banish black from your working life.

If you treat black with the respect it deserves, it will repay you by endowing you with all the glamour and mystery of a first lady or film star.

black

white

dove gray

steel gray

bitter chocolate

"I can't wear black on its own. I wish I could. But I can wear it with my grandmother's fur stole."

" You might not think that you suit a certain color, but there will always be a shade that will suit you. Don't be lazy and only wear color with black; open up your imagination and wear color with color. **"**

S̄

04
Culling

Look in your wardrobe and what do you see? Rows of clothes you wear every day because you love them all, each and every item? Neatly hung garments that hold your admiration because they all look fabulous on your form? Like hell you do. We bet millions that the more likely scenario is one of shelves littered with clothes that haven't been worn in eons.

Don't think we don't know about the knickers that have grayed in the wash and can't stand up for themselves because the elastic has gone. Don't lie about those sweaters. We know they're all full of holes. Oh Lord! Now look at those dresses. They haven't seen daylight in years, but their garish color schemes have not faded at all. And check out the shoes. You know full well that you will never get that heel fixed and the scuffed toes of your boots are beyond polish salvation. Your first boyfriend may have given you the spray-on jodhpurs with suede patches. They remain hideous and you can't even get into them. Sure, your navy winter coat cost a week's wages and has a designer label, but that doesn't take away its exaggerated lapel and dandruff-embedded shoulders.

When your hair gets too long and the ends become split-ridden you get it cut. If your appendix explodes you have it surgically removed. Well, the same has to be done with your clothes. What is the point of cluttering up your closets with things that are never worn, be it for sentimental reasons or financial ones? If they aren't worn, they aren't worn. Get rid of the buggers.

Culling is relevant to every stage of a woman's life, and particularly for women going through menopause, who may hold on to clothing from the time they felt their most feminine and sexy. Get these clothes out of your wardrobe; they will only depress you. And then you can get something new to replace them.

If you are looking to meet Mr. Right, get rid of those clothes that make you look like you've always got your period. You never know when you are going to meet him so even the most casual outfit must be well thought-out. Mr. Right might be walking down the supermarket aisle.

Because a good culling is no easy task, it does help to have a friend harden your resolve. And she will persuade you to get rid of those leather trousers that sag at the bum. All is not lost, however, because those less fortunate than you can benefit from the funds raised by selling those old skirts and jackets in charity shops, and your appearance will benefit from newer and more expensive things being sold to raise funds for a shopping spree.

Bagging old clothes is like casting out baggage from your past. It is a cathartic process that will make you feel cleansed and renewed. And there is no downside to culling because for every six or so items you discard there will be another you find among the rubble that can be worn with the pride of a spanking new purchase.

While some pieces deserve nothing better than a garbage bag, others could look good among the charmingly dated merchandise unique to charity shops. These you'll get no cash for (obviously), but send the more with-it items to a secondhand store and your financial reapings could be significant enough to buy a new coat. Anything over a decade old, in good order and preferably with a designer label attached will find a wealthy home on eBay or in a vintage shop. Making money from your cast-offs eases the agony of saying good-bye to old friends (even if they have been stabbing you in the back by making you look ghastly).

Go back to the war zone that is your wardrobe, take a deep breath and dive in.

BRAS

We bet that there are more redundant bras in your drawers than anything else. This is because your bust is more susceptible to size fluctuation than any other part of your body. Think of pre-period, pregnancy and weight gain or loss. Fit is immeasurably important. If your boobs spill over the top, the straps dig into your skin, it's turned gray, the underwire is poking out or it is nothing more than a nipple shield, chuck it.

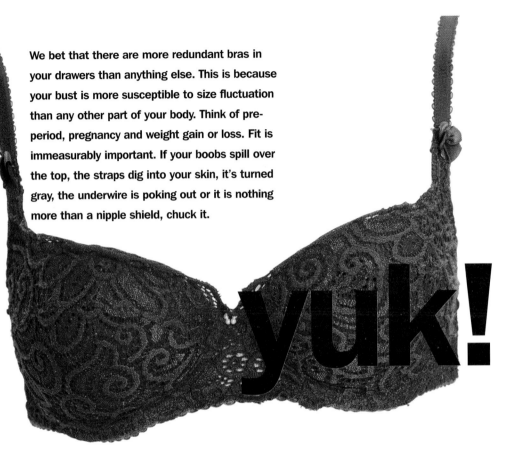

yuk!

UNDERWEAR

The g-string gives VPL freedom. Low-waisted boy shorts are great for jeans, but bikini briefs and cami-panties along with any granny panties aren't flattering and can go, together with anything discolored or gaping with loose elastic. If your pants are clean, fresh and invisible, *you* are clean, fresh and confident.

SWIMWEAR

Try on all your swimwear and get rid of any orphan pieces, anything that doesn't fit or is stretched beyond redemption. If your body has been ravaged by childbirth, maybe it's time to put two pieces behind you. A smart one piece can look wonderful.

SWEATERS

The culling candidates here are numerous. And also the hardest because a sweater is warm even if it is peppered with moth holes. But it will be better given to Goodwill. A sweater should always have shape, no matter what your size.

T-SHIRTS

We always need that holiday souvenir and the pop concert memory. We need one to go with jeans, one for under a jacket. Some for exercising, some for sleeping. Whatever, we all have far too many. You don't need the baggy, the too-tight white or the one attacked by red boxer shorts in the wash. Stick to T-shirts that suit your shape, a few white, a few colors and motifs. Ten should suffice.

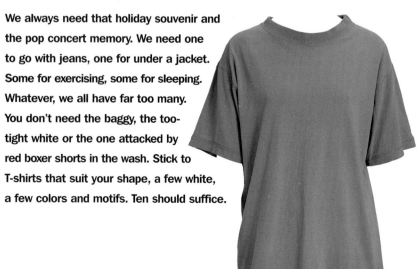

SKIRTS

Being more of a headline garment, skirts are harder to dump. To be honest, once you have found your favored shape there really should be no need to eject them unless the hardware has been hit, like a zipper or a hook and eye. Summer holiday skirts (gorgeous colors and wafting fabrics) can go on forever. Get rid of anything that's been splashed by wine, anything that's too short or requires a slip, and most definitely anything with an elastic or gathered waist.

in the

TOPS

Other top-half garments that should be tossed: the classic but-no-longer-white shirt, the silk top (fine for flat chests or the mature lady) and halternecks (unless you have the skin of a 12-year-old). Keep vests well hidden when they're out of fashion.

bin please!

We feel a short coat is a better investment than a jacket, unless it's a useful waterproof or sportscoat. The price is usually much the same, and it's a more modern look. Toss anything that has even the remotest sheen from too much dry cleaning, anything with big shoulders or a blouson style, and certainly bomber and biker jackets – sooo unflattering. Leather jackets can stay if they are fitted, and jean jackets (the older the better) too, unless they are stonewashed.

HATS

These are probably in competition with your oldest bras for the least-used items in your wardrobe. By all means keep your favorite sun and sporting hats. All the others that have been gathering dust at the top of your wardrobe should go – the picture hat, the beret, the trilby and anything you bought in the eighties and haven't worn since. That doesn't mean you shouldn't wear hats; just reevaluate what suits you, and update. There is never a reason to wear a baseball cap.

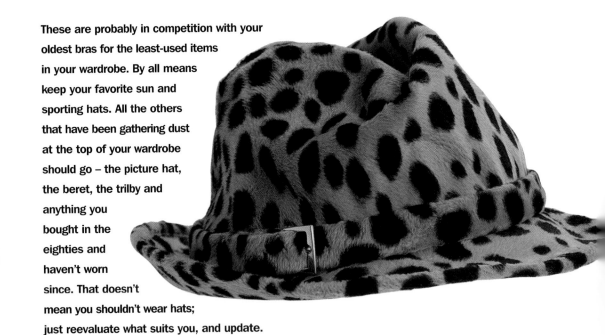

TROUSERS

Our least favorite trouser has pleats at the waist and tapered legs that end at the ankle. And it's usually black too. Get rid of it, or them, immediately. And toss any jeans that are stonewashed, drainpipe, studded or way too tight. You've probably got several pairs you no longer wear taking up valuable space in your wardrobe.

If you live in a cold climate you will wear this item proportionately more often than any other in your wardrobe, so think about updating it accordingly. If you have the perfect coat that's simple, stylish and elegant, then look after it, along with the stylish vintage evening coat if you are lucky enough to have one. Anything that's shapeless, moth-eaten or worn should go.

eeek!

"Make do and mend'

Second World War poster campaign

Only if there's a war on.

SCARVES

Shawls, cashmere pashminas and realistic imitation fur scarves are warm and therefore have a purpose. Everything else needs close inspection before you consider keeping it. There's absolutely no reason to keep the thin velvet or chiffon scarf, the synthetic "angora," the chenille, and alas, the square silk scarf presently out of fashion for anyone except the elegant older woman.

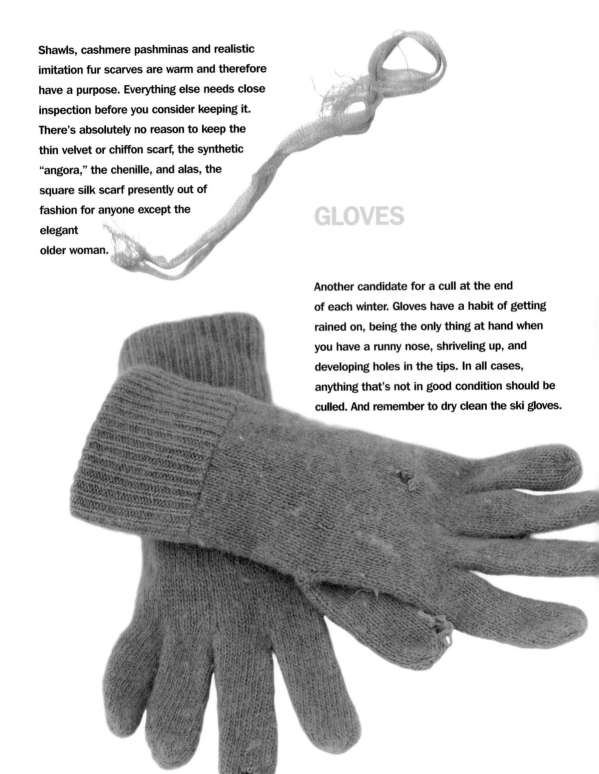

GLOVES

Another candidate for a cull at the end of each winter. Gloves have a habit of getting rained on, being the only thing at hand when you have a runny nose, shriveling up, and developing holes in the tips. In all cases, anything that's not in good condition should be culled. And remember to dry clean the ski gloves.

SHOES

If it's too small, too high or uncomfortable, there's a heel missing or the leather is terminally scraped, the inner sole is buckling or, worse still, it smells, out it goes. The same applies to ancient sneakers and those expensive evening shoes that don't go with anything in your wardrobe.

And check that what you keep is the right shape for your leg.

BAGS

We don't believe in the bag-for-each-outfit way of thinking, but we do believe the one-bag-for-all-occasions is completely wrong. The kitchen sink bag is unsightly and bad for your back. It's time to wave good-bye to some other old friends too – anything that lives out of sight (and out of mind) in the top of the closet, anything that's stained, frayed or just plain dirty, as well as anything that is quilted, has a gold chain or was a makeup freebie.

EVENING GOWN

It cost a fortune at the time and you have worn it twice (the last time being ten years ago). It's sexy, but a little tight, or a bit too short. It's got frills or eighties beading. If any of the above apply, it's out. If there's something you really love and it looks great but is stained, try having it dyed a darker color.

scary!

DRESSES

Our least favorite is the raucously colored dress that ties at the back and makes you look like a sack of potatoes. Uggh. Be ruthless and cull the mistakes you made looking for the right-shaped dress in the right colors for you.

Most of us have boxes of impulse buys dating back to our teens, and much of what's in them doesn't stand up to scrutiny today. If you haven't bothered to replace the missing stone

or restring the broken necklace, out it should go. Any intact pieces can go into the children's dressing-up box or to charity. Keep the charm bracelets for the next generation.

"Don't do this alone. Make sure you have a friend to harden your resolve. If she's not your shape, so much the better - or she will want the clothes."

05
No-cost
wardrobe

This chapter is most relevant for women with toddlers and teenagers. Because you are always thinking of giving everything to the kids, there is nothing left in the piggy bank for yourself. Stop just being a mom. You are still a wife or partner, and it's important that you don't dress just for practicality. You may not be able to afford new clothes, so this is the ideal solution.

One assumes increasing the contents of one's wardrobe means spending money on new clothes. Over the years, however, we have discovered that many of the clothes worn by us actually look better on friends whose body parts are correctly developed to take a certain shape or style of clothing. You may desire the asset of another woman, but woe betide that physical trophy if it's adorned in something it doesn't suit. The enlarged chest Trinny may desire will look awful in a turtleneck, but because she is as flat as a freshly pressed ski slope, the roll-neck sweater becomes an altogether more elegant item upon her torso whereas it is not a possibility for Susannah.

In the old days we were always buying clothes that were better for each other. It took a while for the penny to drop that Susannah looked atrocious in the strappy dresses Trinny encouraged her to buy. This wasn't evil intent on Trin's part. She genuinely loved the dresses. When Susannah, enchanted by killer heels with ankle cuffs, implored Trinny to take them, this was not a secret stab in the back, but a desire to see Trinny as happy as she would have been could her bank balance have absorbed the price tag. Back in those days we were ignorant of the fact that what was captivating to one of us was cataclysmic when put on the other. Once the bulb lit, we began swapping clothes.

This very basic fact leads to an extremely profitable plan in terms of gathering clothes for nothing. Invite a bunch of girlfriends over for dinner along with a selection of their clothes. Try on each other's items. Be ruthless in your assessments (especially if criticizing something you know will look better on you). Things that don't suit you can be donated to a properly shaped friend in exchange for something of hers you look great in and she doesn't.

This exchange should not be about labels and prices. In order to make the event equal and not about money, each girl should remove the labels of her clothes before she attends the party. This will also make people desire the clothes rather than the label and make objective choices. It's an obvious idea, but a good one that really does allow you to walk away with some new outfits without a single penny exchanging hands.

This is especially good for friends who might have a vast wardrobe that could come winging your way, but it is equally satisfying to help a friend with less money than you without making her feel like a charity case.

You might also be hanging on to your thinner-day clothing in the vain hope that one day it will fit you again. Let it go in the knowledge that what goes around comes around, and if and when you lose that weight, the universe will always provide.

Swapping clothes is also a great way to obtain and get rid of a pregnancy wardrobe. You won't feel so guilty about the black-tie dress you spent a fortune on and only wore when you were pregnant.

You might be holding on to an item because of its sentimental value; if you love it so much, give it a new lease on life and see the joy it gives to a friend rather than let it hang unworn in your closet. At the end of the day it's about friendship.

Every woman has screaming mistakes in her wardrobe that she tries to ignore by pushing them into the back recesses where they fester in the vain hope of being worn. It's never going to happen, so appease your guilt and get rid of them NOW.

" If you've wear

got it, it"

Lord Mountbatten

But if it looks better on your best friend, give it to her. $\overline{s}$

List of friends

_____

_____

_____

_____

_____

_____

_____

_____

_____

_____

_____

_____

_____

_____

Things I would like to get rid of:

_____

_____

_____

_____

_____

Things I would like to get:

_____

_____

_____

_____

_____

"We all know retail therapy is the best kind, but there will always be times when we can't afford it. You don't have to spend money to get new clothes. "

06
Acces

The quickest and most effective way to accomplish a stylish appearance is with accessories. But like anything that works wonders, there is no shortcut to learning how to accessorize well.

While we have always said style isn't innate, there are women to whom the art of knowing how to use accessories comes easily. They will inherently know which shoes to put with a particular length of skirt and how a necklace can make or break an outfit. Those of us deprived of the accessory gene need to be taught what to do.

Deciding which types of accessories suit you depends very much on the shape and size of your bones. Forget about how much you weigh for once – it is your bones we want to focus on.

Look at us as an example. Susannah is pudgier than Trinny (except on her arse), but because she is fine boned, she is more suited to delicate accessories. Thin Trin, on the other hand, is blessed with heftier bones that can carry off bold accessories, which in turn stand out more.

While we admit this bone thing is, of course, a sweeping generalization, and there are always exceptions to the rule, it's a starting point to a subject that will change your attitude to dressing.

How on earth can you tell what is a big or a small bone? Well, the difference isn't enormous. We are not talking brontosaurus excavation site versus wren skeleton here. No, the definition is more subtle. Look at your wrists and ankles and if these are proportionately delicate to the rest of your arms and legs, then your bones are small. If, however, the two are less distinct and you have, for example, thick ankles, your prize is that you can wear fabulously daring pieces that people comment on. Hands, too, are a strong indicator to sizing accessories. Do your fingers look better in big or small rings?

Personality plays a part as well. No shrinking violet, however enormous her bones, is going to want to stand out with an accessory that screams, "Look at me!"

The bottom line is that big characters have the balls to go bold or fragile, whereas the reserved may want to play it safe with subtlety.

Think the learning process stops here? Well, interestingly, clothes do play a part, too, especially when it comes to color. Keeping your accessories in tune with what you wear is vital, however important a piece is. The thing you love most about an outfit may be the necklace that you wear with it because it is such an individual item. Even in this instance, your clothes need to be of a similar coloring but of an unfussy fabric and pattern that will make the necklace stand out. The tone you set also makes a difference. Diamanté in the daytime looks cheap, but it comes into its own at night.

We also firmly believe less is more. Someone who wears her entire jewelry collection about her person does not look rich and classy but desperate to be *seen* as rich and classy.

It might be that the season's hottest look is military or flamenco. Unless you have either a boyish form or a curvaceous Latin American one, you can't go there in terms of clothes.

You can, however, make great use of a gold button or two, or the rose that looks so good on a Spanish dancer in full regalia; it would look just as wonderful pinned to the lapel of your jacket.

Once you know your style, but want to be fashionable, give more attention to the runway shoe when looking through glossy magazines. You can pick up super-trendy footwear from stores like Zara at a fraction of the cost of the originals.

BEST BAGS

A woman can never get away with just one "useful bag." What will she do when she goes to the ball, wears different colored clothes, gets on a plane or goes down to the beach? There are many occasions when we need a bag, and for each of these we should have at least one example. So if you are that girl who owns only a practical navy shoulder bag, it's off to the shops you must go.

Here is your list for an ideal bag collection.

- Day bag in brown. This will be worn with all colors apart from black, although ideally we would like you to get a few different colors.

- Day bag in black. Not as useful, funnily enough, as the brown, because you can only wear it with black, white, gray or taupe.

- Funky fabric bag. Dotted with a few beads or flowers, this is great for playtime and when you're going out for dinner.

- Evening bag. Best to get this to match up with your jewelry. If you like diamonds, get a silver bag, and if you are a gold girl, get a gold one.

- Travel bag. One that will fit in the overhead locker of a plane. This will double up as a weekend bag.

- Beach bag. Preferably lined in something that can be wiped clean when your sun cream leaks or water seeps into it.

- No-bag bag. A bag that is little more than a wallet for the days when you need to carry only the bare essentials, like keys, card and phone.

BAGS

It is so easy to ruin an outfit with the wrong bag. So many women assume that one bag fits all. It truly doesn't. Heavy, dark-colored bags may look fine with your winter coat but they will overwhelm a floaty summer outfit. And you don't always want to carry your practical workday number on the weekend.

Below left Susannah's bag is nice enough, but dull and mumsy.
Below The novel shape of this bag adds an element of fun.

Opposite left The heavy black bag completely swamps Trinny's dress.
Opposite The pink bag is prettier and more in proportion with Trinny and the dress.

KITCHEN SINK BAG

A busy woman needs to carry her life in her bag, so it needs to be big if it's going to hold the contents of her daily routine. It might rain, so there's an umbrella. She might be called upon for a sudden meeting so there's her calendar and notebook. She might have to dash straight from the office to the dinner table, so there's the hefty makeup kit to reapply her face. Murphy's law she'll have her period at the same time. Her big bristly hairbrush will also be included because it's the only one she has. If she has children, there will probably be a stray diaper or half-empty bottle of baby milk in there, too. All that's missing is the proverbial kitchen sink, but of course there's no room for that.

If you are that woman, it's time to think mini. Buy small sizes of makeup and beauty products or decant them into miniature containers. The brush can be shrunk to a few inches that will do the job just as effectively as the big fella. Cull all unnecessary items. You can get tiny, light umbrellas, and how about an electronic organizer instead of a heavyweight one?

What a joy it will be to have easy access to your life by getting rid of the chaos that was once the contents of your handbag.

Below Before and after handbags.

Above Contents of the kitchen sink bag.
Right Revamped mini contents for the new, organized you.

SCARVES

Scarves, believe it or not, come in many different guises and can give off a variety of impressions. You can make any scarf look funky – or old ladyish.

The answer to good scarf-wearing lies in the way it is tied. A silken square knotted far back under the chin can immediately turn a young woman into a walker-pushing old dear who smokes 50 cigarettes a day. The very same scarf knotted ON the chin belongs to a horse and hounder whose fashion role model is Princess Anne. If this same silken square is worn as a wide headband from the hairline back, around a pair of jeans, or tied to a Marc Jacobs-style bag next to worry beads or a cool key ring, it suddenly becomes non-stereotypical and rather hip.

A few hints on scarf wearing:

• Look out for unique scarves in vintage stores.

• A Missoni scarf can teach you about color because this design house really understands how to combine complementary hues.

• If you are short and yearn for a long scarf, don't be lured into wearing one in a thick knit; opt for a lightweight material or woven silk.

• A scarf is fab worn as a belt with jeans.

- If your hair needs a wash, cover it up in a scarf worn hairband style à la Elizabeth Taylor in the sixties.
- Short necks must wear scarves wrapped around the neck to create an elongating turtleneck effect.
- Long necks can wear scarves looped and tied.
- Scarves folded in a triangle and placed over the shoulders like a cowl are very mumsy.
- A cotton kerchief tied around the neck and worn with a T-shirt makes for a fresh French feel that works for all ages and is a nice alternative to the hideously tied Sailor Boy knot.
- The scarf worn like a choker is the savior of wrinkly turkey necks.

Opposite left Susannah's scarf is wildly out of proportion with her size.
Opposite right The scaled-down version, wrapped around her neck, is the right size and a good style for a shorter neck.

Below A kerchief tied this way might have been smart in the nineties, but then, as now, it disappears on Trinny.
Right With her longer neck, Trinny can wear a thick scarf looped and tied.

BELTS

It's all a question of position and width with belts. We are no longer expected to wear leather belts in the day, leaving the fancy ones for night. Anything goes at any time, especially when the belt concerned is worn with jeans. There is no point in even considering a belt before you have worked out the ideal place for your waistline. That is, does your pot belly require a waistband that cuts across it or is your bottom

skinny little belt!

so large it needs to be halved by a hipster waistband?

Width of belt and buckle size can make a difference to a belt looking cool or not. Wearing a belt that hits a dodgy part of your torso will double the deformity by drawing attention to it.

BELTS

A few hints on belts.

- If you are small boned, keep the buckle small or delicate, even if you're overweight.

- Those with dinosaur bones can go for bust with bold, big, chunky buckles.

- But they don't look great in thin belts, even if they are super-skinny.

- When you are wearing one color head to toe, don't break it up with a different colored belt.

Below left A waisted belt only emphasizes and enlarges Trinny's bottom half.
Below Trinny looks best in a bold belt with a large buckle that rests on her hips.

- You can wear funky buckles with everything as long as you keep the belt monochrome.
- Big boobs don't look great with big belts, because it all becomes too complicated.
- Short waists, too, must beware of wide belts because they eat up what waist you do have, giving the illusion that your boobs hang low enough to touch your middle.
- Long backs must wear belts low to stop their butt from looking too big from the back.

Below left The same big buckle does no favors for Susannah, especially when it's at waist level.
Below A slightly smaller buckle with the belt resting on her hips flatters Susannah's curvaceous shape.

NECKLACES

Jesus, what a shocker Susannah's face is in that necklace. Even without the necklace it is a horrifying example of age catching up like a stealth bomber. One doesn't often see oneself from this angle and our first piece of advice is to avoid the side-mirror view. It has forced Susannah into thinking it might be time for Botox.

The beauty of necklaces is that they need not be heirlooms to lift an outfit from the bottom step of mediocrity to the highest echelons of a Best Dresser. Look at Audrey Hepburn in *Breakfast at Tiffany's* or Jackie O in the White House; they both understood the power of a plain dress teamed with a fabulous necklace.

Left Susannah's short neck should not be encased in a dog collar–style necklace, nor should non-matching earrings be competing with the necklace.

Below Susannah and Trinny in necklaces that are perfect for their body shape and size.

NECKLACES

The bottom line is that if you have a short neck, squat face or big boobs, or if you are in any way unfortunate enough to resemble Susannah, then necklaces should be one of the lesser items in your accessory collection. Unhappily short necks, especially necks with a suggestion of a double or triple chin, look terrible in necklaces.

• Long necks are easy to strangle because they look fab in chokers, chunky pieces and long, dangly jeweled wreaths. They are genetically bred to wear necklaces, although even they have their limitations.

• Look at the neckline of your top as well as the tone of your outfit before deciding which beaded collar to wear. Slash-neck styles are barred from necklaces...do earrings instead.

• Big boobs cannot do long and dangly because the line of the necklace becomes distorted once it hits the chest.

• Short necks are best entwined by delicate pieces that don't take up too much space between the chin and the breasts.

• Sloping, padded-with-fat shoulders are best suited to necklaces that are fine and filamented

Above Susannah's short neck and big boobs compete for attention with this chunky necklace.

with small beads; angular, architectural necklaces need a good pair of coat-hanger shoulders to carry them off.

• Flat chests are wonderful boards on which to rest a huge show-stopping piece that can reach as low as your belly button.

• Never wear lots of gold chains together unless you are a rap star.

• As you will only be wearing a turtleneck with a flat chest, a long necklace that is bold and flamboyant is the S & T-approved option. Chains and pendants over turtlenecks look cheap.

• Long necks look weak and giraffelike when circled by a thin choker. They can carry something much wider and look amazing in it.

• A long neck coming out of a round-neck top looks fabulous with a big chunky necklace at collarbone level.

• Don't wear an over-the-top necklace and wild earrings together unless they are part of a set.

• Big boobs can carry off a delicate droplet necklace that ends just at the top of the cleavage. Never allow a pendant to disappear into a cleavage ravine.

Above The right necklace for Susannah is delicate, thus extending the length of her neck and not competing with other features.

"**It's what you leave off a dress that makes it smart**

Nettie Rosenstein

On the contrary, clever use of a decorative touch can transform a cheap-looking outfit into an expensive-looking one.

EARRINGS

How can anyone create fashion frisson with a pair of earrings? Surely these are the one accessory immune to style flu? Unfortunately we know otherwise. Bad earring-wearing habits appear to be spreading all over the country. Wide gold hoops engraved with fancy twirly lines worn next to a small gold hoop, next to a stud, is very popular, very pedestrian and very ugly. Pearl studs are fab worn with ultra ladylike clothes, but become uninspiring and dull when worn all the time.

Amazingly, the shape of one's face, the length of the neck and how many chins you own have a huge impact on the shape of earrings that are right for you. You'd expect your hairstyle to be important too, but it's not. Same with clothing. Obviously mega-diamonds with galoshes and a raincoat is odd (unless you're naked underneath), but generally the more unexpected the pairing, the better it looks.

• Long faces look good in chandelier-shaped earrings and they're able to carry off a stud.

what are those?

• Round and dangly earrings will make a fatter face and chin look thinner.

• Round faces and hanging chins should stay away from studs or circular clip-ons.

• Short necks become even shorter next to long, dangly earrings that hang to the shoulder.

• If a short neck or small face wants to do discreet, opt for small, plain gold or silver hoops rather than studs.

• Plain golf-ball–sized hoops suit everyone.

• If the colors of your earrings complement your outfit they can be as sparkly as you like, even for the day.

• Cool earrings can transform a plain Jane.

• Don't wear fancy, dangly earrings if you want to look professional and relatively serious. Better to go for a great bracelet, brooch or necklace.

• Diamanté looks wonderful when it is full-on, over the top, but not so hot as when it's trying to be a diamond stud. The latter looks like something fake trying to be real whereas a chandelier earring celebrates its false origins.

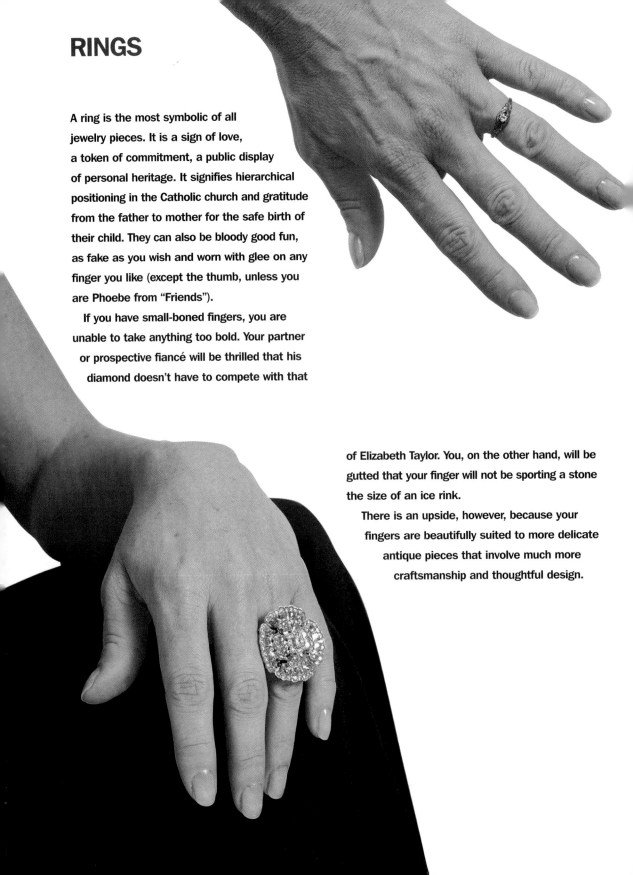

RINGS

A ring is the most symbolic of all jewelry pieces. It is a sign of love, a token of commitment, a public display of personal heritage. It signifies hierarchical positioning in the Catholic church and gratitude from the father to mother for the safe birth of their child. They can also be bloody good fun, as fake as you wish and worn with glee on any finger you like (except the thumb, unless you are Phoebe from "Friends").

If you have small-boned fingers, you are unable to take anything too bold. Your partner or prospective fiancé will be thrilled that his diamond doesn't have to compete with that of Elizabeth Taylor. You, on the other hand, will be gutted that your finger will not be sporting a stone the size of an ice rink.

There is an upside, however, because your fingers are beautifully suited to more delicate antique pieces that involve much more craftsmanship and thoughtful design.

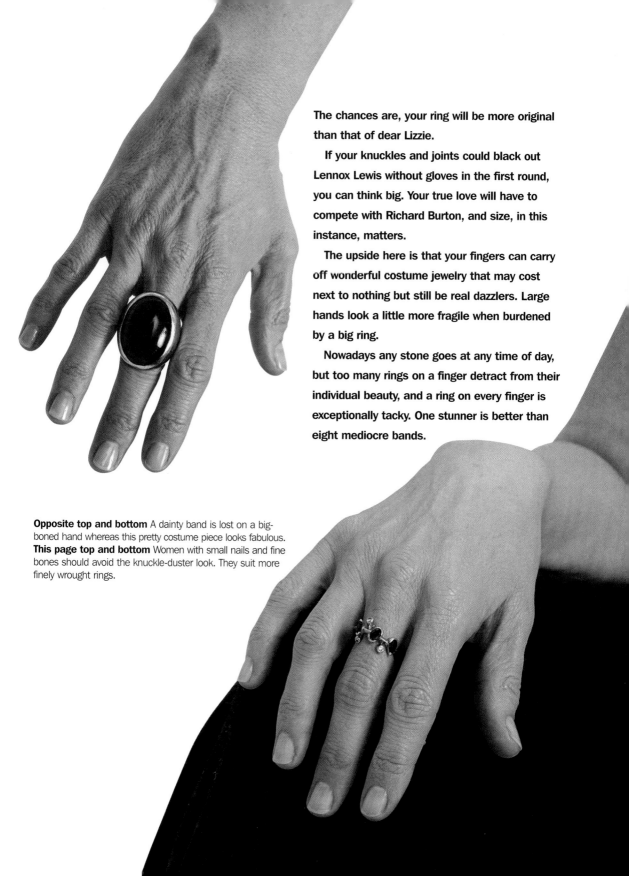

The chances are, your ring will be more original than that of dear Lizzie.

If your knuckles and joints could black out Lennox Lewis without gloves in the first round, you can think big. Your true love will have to compete with Richard Burton, and size, in this instance, matters.

The upside here is that your fingers can carry off wonderful costume jewelry that may cost next to nothing but still be real dazzlers. Large hands look a little more fragile when burdened by a big ring.

Nowadays any stone goes at any time of day, but too many rings on a finger detract from their individual beauty, and a ring on every finger is exceptionally tacky. One stunner is better than eight mediocre bands.

Opposite top and bottom A dainty band is lost on a big-boned hand whereas this pretty costume piece looks fabulous. **This page top and bottom** Women with small nails and fine bones should avoid the knuckle-duster look. They suit more finely wrought rings.

BRACELETS

A bracelet is a great present for yourself or for a girlfriend. If it's someone you loathe, but are obliged to give to, like a hateful sister-in-law, just buy her the wrong shape. She will be delighted. The subtlety of its inappropriateness will be lost on her.

Bracelets are the only piece of jewelry that can look great en masse. It doesn't look cheap to have 20 bangles on your arm, just as long as they are all from the same family. Think of an Indian woman, beautiful in her sari, her arms ringed by scores of thin gold bangles; they look wonderful. Then think of an arm dripping with clunky gold charm bracelets, various-sized chains and the odd bangle, and the image isn't quite so pleasing.

Left Trinny, having a larger bone structure, can wear a chunky bracelet; the diamanté bracelet is lost on her arm.

Opposite On Susannah, the heavier bracelet makes her arm look chubby, while a more delicate style gives a slim and elegant look.

Unless gold and silver is in the same bracelet as a design feature, don't put these two metals together. They try to outshine each other and end up looking lackluster.

• You've guessed it: small bones are better off with delicate bracelets whereas bigger wrists are able to carry off something much chunkier.

• Wearing two identical cuffs on each arm is a sophisticated method of achieving instant style.

• Buy lots of the same cheap bracelet and wear them all together for a lush look.

• A bracelet worn with a watch can be pretty as long as it doesn't overpower the timepiece and looks like it never need come off.

• Secondhand and charity shops are brilliant foraging grounds for retro pieces.

SHOES THICK ANKLES FLAT

For those with thick ankles, flat shoes with a thin toe make the ankle look even stumpier. A high ankle strap strangles the ankle, and a low kitten heel is in danger of looking like it's going to snap under your weight.

A more substantial shoe looks in proportion to a more substantial ankle so a chunky loafer is a good choice. A simple thong lends much-needed length to a thick ankle, and clogs are a thick ankle's best friend.

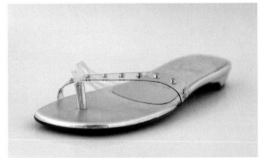

These shoes would make thick ankles look truly titanic.

Shoes to turn shapeless ankles into a respectable part of the body

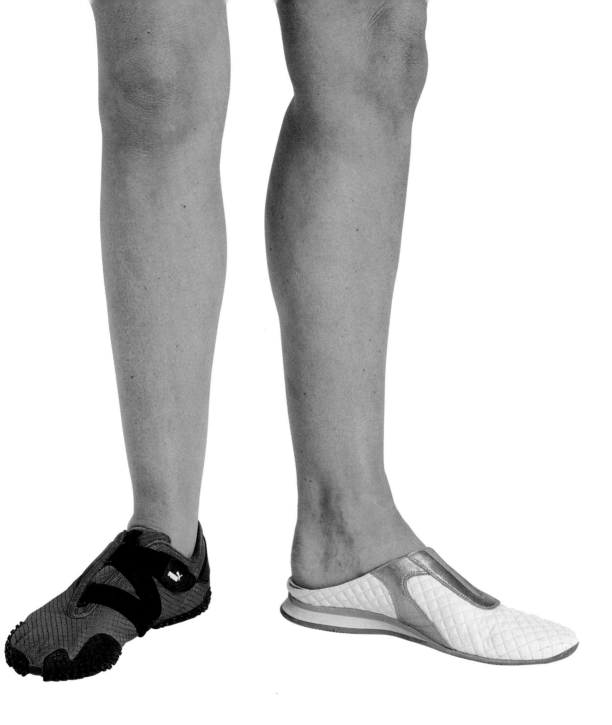

A full sneaker will make the leg look short and stubby.

A flat mule elongates the leg, giving the appearance of a thin ankle.

SHOES THICK ANKLES HEELS

Those with thick ankles will find that a heeled shoe with a high back cuts into and covers up the thinnest part of the ankle, thus making matters worse. Slingbacks with kitten heels and mules with a thin heel will both look like you have squashed a large leg into a tiny shoe.

If you wear a pump, make sure the heel comes straight down from the base of the shoe, which will give your ankle some shape. A slingback can look good with a high, sturdy heel and a heavy heel on a wedge mule will make your ankles appear thinner.

Delicate heels exaggerate a thick ankle.

These styles flatter and distract attention from your ankles.

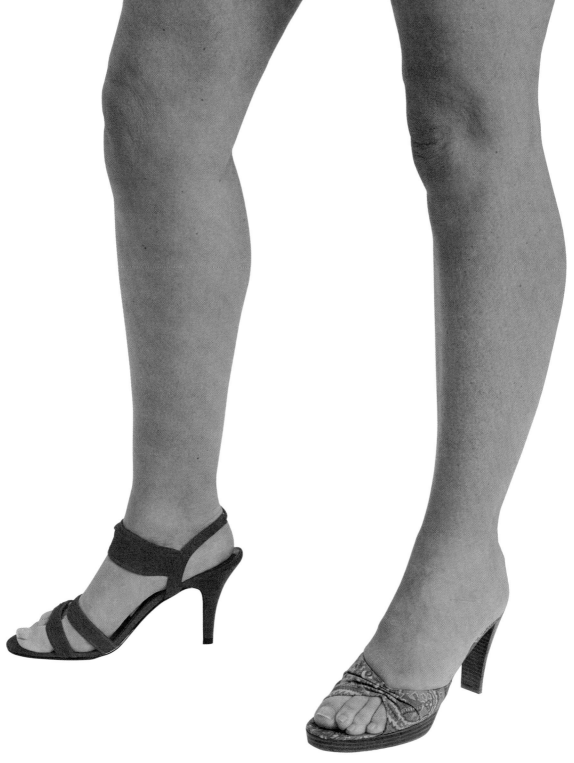

The ankle strap cuts off the length of the foot and takes the eye to the least flattering part of the leg.

The low cut of this shoe draws the eye down and away from the ankle.

SHOES THIN ANKLES FLAT

Thin ankles will look like trees stuck in concrete in clumpy shoes such as Birkenstock clogs. Even a ballet flat will appear to swamp the foot, and large details, such as flowers, tend to overpower a thin ankle.

If you wear an open-backed shoe it needs to be a thong sandal so the flow of your leg isn't broken. Pointed toes finish off the ankle in a less jarring way than a round toe. Any detail in the front of the shoe should be delicate.

These shoes will only emphasize a skinny ankle and leg.

But these styles help sylph-like ankles look their best.

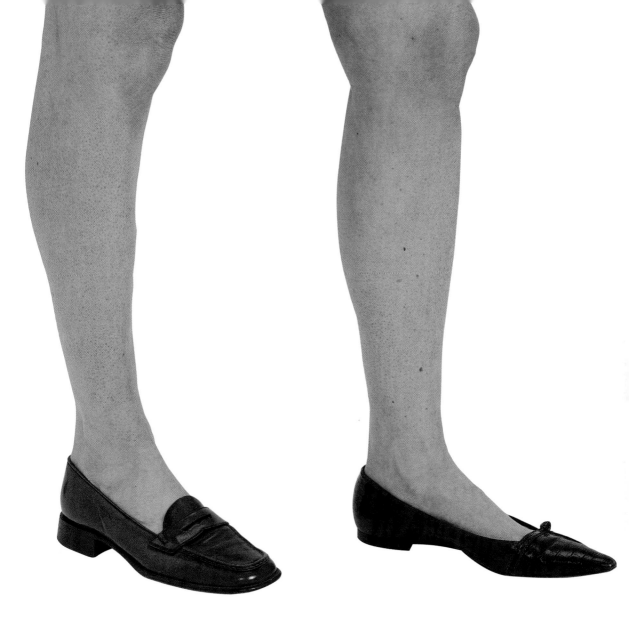

The high front and chunky heel of this style of shoe are too heavy for a delicate ankle.

A pointed toe with a slim heel will flatter the leg.

SHOES THIN ANKLES HEELS

Beware of hefty heels if you are blessed with thin ankles. They dominate the shoe, make your feet look enormous and exaggerate the skinniness of your ankles.

More elegant heels will allow the wearer to show off her ankles to best advantage without the shoes detracting from them and drawing too much attention to her feet.

If your ankles are dainty, shoes like these will make your feet look enormous.

The shoe styles above are much more flattering for a slender ankle.

When wearing ankle straps, the usual rules apply – a slender heel is much more flattering to a thin ankle than a chunky heel.

BOOTS

We work with countless numbers of women who shy away from skirts because they are ashamed of their legs.

We say: "That's why boots were invented."

They say: "My calves are too big and I can't get a boot on."

We reply: "Have you tried the pull-on version?"

They haven't.

We say: "You'll get them over your legs and they will be your passport to ever-after skirt wearing."

They give it a go and suddenly a new world of dressing opens up.

If you have ankles that really should be hidden, the boot allows you to wear skirts of all lengths. Boots have saved thousands of women from a lifetime in trousers. This doesn't mean, however, that dainty legs are privileged in being able to wear every type of boot. They can't, and a thin calf can look just as dodgy in the wrong boot as a thick one does in a skirt.

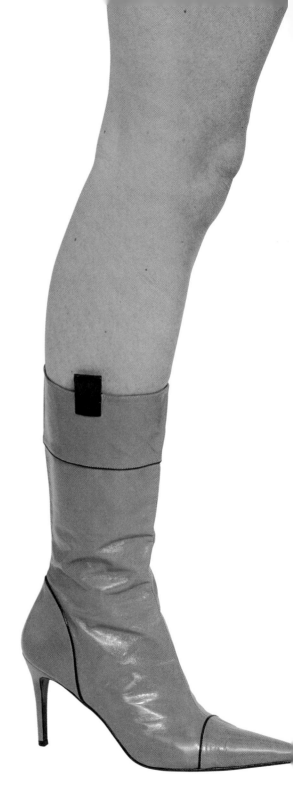

- **Thin legs can look like sticks in pull-on boots if they are too loose around the calf.**
- **Big boobs need a thicker heel on their boot to balance the body shape.**
- **Try to avoid having a gap between the top of your boot and your skirt.**
- **If you do, fill it with fun tights, like fishnets.**
- **Don't tuck your trousers into a pair of ankle boots. You'll look like a pantomime character.**
- **If zip-ups just won't zip up your chunky calf, buy pull-ons. They will seem to take inches off your ankles.**
- **Thin legs look great in heel-free boots; fat legs don't.**

Opposite If you are cursed with chunky calves, calf-length boots will only emphasize your problem.
Left Finding a boot that totally encases your lower leg is the best way to distract attention from chunky calves.

"Accessories can make or break an outfit. Apart from a few exceptions it is better to tone rather than match exactly."

s

07
Storage

When Trinny is in a foul mood, Susannah can guarantee her wardrobe has been hit by a tornado. A relaxed and composed Trinny springs from beautifully rearranged shelves (again) that look like something only Mother Nature could create with such precision.

Extraordinary, don't you think, that a tidy wardrobe can have such an effect. Susannah always laughed at her partner's anal-retentiveness. "I mean, how utterly puerile. The girl is spitting hatpins because her wardrobe is a bit untidy. She should see mine!"

The fact of the matter was that Susannah was reduced to a pulp of quivering frustration every morning because her outfit searching was like beating a path through virgin rain forest. Her life was severely hampered and compromised because she was too lazy to order her clothes. A big day meant finding and trying on endless clothes the night before the event. The consequence of which was less story time for the kids or an enraged husband yelling at her to get a move on.

There will no doubt be many of you who identify with Susannah. Your wardrobes will be bursting at the seams but there is nothing to wear. When you are running late all your decent clothes cower at the back of the closet. Trousers huddle in one corner, shirts in another. Jackets hide under coats. You negotiate with what you can find then beg them to look fabulous. They never do.

A life-changing event such as a new baby makes the situation even worse as your house is overtaken by tiny clothes and toys. It's imperative to ensure your storage space is well ordered if you don't want to spend the rest of your life in chaos.

If your wardrobe is a mess you assume you are bereft of things you actually have. You go shopping. Spend more money. Then find its twin back in the wardrobe. It was there all the time. This is when you think, "Okay, I'd better have a tidy-up." A swift swipe of organization and you think you have changed the world. The wardrobe looks neater, yes. But its contents remain a mystery. Why? Well, nothing has been hung or put away with an ounce of intelligence.

You need a brain to tidy clothes? No. But the method of Trinny's madness you do need. It sounds crazy, but perfectly displayed clothing will have a huge impact on your day and save you loads of time, especially if you store winter clothes elsewhere in the summer.

Less to choose from also makes for sharper decision-making. What's the point of having lovely clothes that suit your body shape if you don't have time to put them together or can't find them? Ordered shelves also start the day with clarity. There is nothing worse than the morning madness of rifling through bits of material that you don't recognize because they are so crumpled. It's more than depressing.

When sorting your clothes in an efficient way it has to be done with forethought and planning. It's not just a question of taking things off wire hangers and putting them on plastic ones. You need to invest in tidiness by buying padded and clip hangers that will make your clothing look beautiful and last longer. The easier it is to see the entire contents of your wardrobe, the easier it is to choose an outfit.

Something so small can waste as much time as the inability to pull together an outfit. Don't just think about the clothes you are wearing; it's the accessories, too, that need to be regimented.

Susannah was unable or perhaps unwilling to turn the corner called "intelligent storage," so it took intervention from her friend. The results since that day have been amazing. Thanks to Trinny's help, Susannah is no longer late and her kids benefit from an entire story at night as opposed to just one chapter.

UNDERWEAR

Organizing your bras, briefs, tights and socks does require some effort, but it's the base on which to build an outfit, and it will save valuable time in the early morning rush hour.

Start by lining your drawers with pretty paper or splurge out and buy cardboard or plastic dividers. You can even use old shoe boxes. And invest in some lavender bags for a good smell.

Then divide your bras and underwear into style and color – everyday, evening and sport.

Keep tights, thigh-highs and stockings separate from socks. And separate dark-colored tights and stockings so you don't confuse them in poor light. Don't put back any that have runs or holes. Socks can be put into categories for style and warmth – cotton, wool, cashmere, walking and sport.

Once you've made the effort to sort everything out, keep it tidy. We never seem to have enough drawer or wardrobe space so finding imaginative methods of storage for all items of clothing is of major importance. The golden rule is to never store anything that is dirty.

Giving the layout of your wardrobe a thorough going-over is almost as therapeutic as a shopping spree. You will meet old friends and team them up in new and imaginative ways.

If you don't have much space available, store out-of-season clothes and shoes in suitcases under the bed. It's worth the effort and a good chance for a seasonal cull.

JEWELRY

Necklaces and bracelets can be hung on wardrobe doors instead of hidden away in boxes where they are hard to find and easy to forget about. They'll look good and seeing them will remind you to wear them more often.

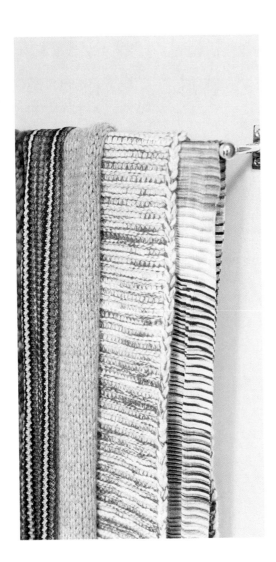

SCARVES

Trinny keeps her scarves folded over a tie rack on the doors of the wardrobe where she stores her tops and sweaters – again, this means she will remember to wear them. They are divided into wool, cashmere and silk.

Scarves can also be folded neatly in small piles according to fabric so you can see the colors easily.

Hats can be stored inside each other in hat boxes with a separating layer of newspaper between each hat.

Belts can be hung together on tie racks or each one placed over the hook of a hanger with the outfit you wear it with.

FOLDING

Being the perfectionist that she is, Trinny stores all her T-shirts, sweats and sweaters in gradations of color, in piles that are not too high and leaves a reasonable space in between each pile. Keep the piles narrow for good visibility, neatness and easy access.

Don't put away a sweater or T-shirt that is dirty. Wash it immediately or take it to the dry cleaners – moths love food-encrusted clothes, and most especially wool and cashmere.

Heavy sweaters can be put away for the summer months – after being hand washed or dry cleaned, then folded in plastic bags. Old dry cleaning covers are ideal for this.

Jeans can be folded and stored on shelves since it doesn't matter if they are a little crushed—in fact they should be.

Scatter your shelves with fragrant cinnamon sticks, cloves or lavender bags to help keep moths at bay.

HANGING

Hanging clothes in an ordered way is the secret to making the most of your wardrobe. We hang as many clothes as we can because it's easier than folding and it's certainly easier to see what you have on hand.

You will need decent hangers – preferably padded, wooden or plastic – for dresses and tops, and clip hangers for trousers and skirts. Hang coats and jackets on wooden hangers.

Banish wire hangers entirely – they cause creasing and unsightly bulges on the shoulders.

When you hang clothes, try to create outfits or group them in colors that go together. Hang camisoles next to cardigans, tops next to a skirt or trousers of a complementary color. Trinny changes the hanging order of her clothes on a regular basis, and always finds an unthought-of match.

Hang trousers from the hem – it will save on ironing.

Put lavender bags on the hangers for a special touch.

"Chaos is a friend of mine

Bob Dylan

And, boy, does it show.

s̄

FOOTWEAR

This part of the wardrobe invariably looks a mess. If you have the space, the ideal solution is a shoe rack. If you don't have the luxury of sufficient space, shoes should be stored in their boxes where they won't gather dust or get lost under a pile of their peers. Attach a polaroid or a photograph to the box for easy identification.

You will need a good cleaning kit and shoe trees to hold the shape. Cedar trees are good for shoes that are inclined to smell; plastic shoe trees are fine for most other shoes.

On the subject of smell: keep shoes that tend to smell and trainers separately. If your shoes get wet, stuff them with newspaper and keep them in a cool, dry place until they are completely dry.

It's a good idea to alternate shoes rather than wear the same pair day after day. They will last a lot longer. And keep them well polished – they look better and the polish will help to repel water.

" It took Susannah ten years to learn from Trinny the benefits of a more anally organized wardrobe. As a result, she feels as if she has more clothes and can spend more time doing other things she knows are important. **"**

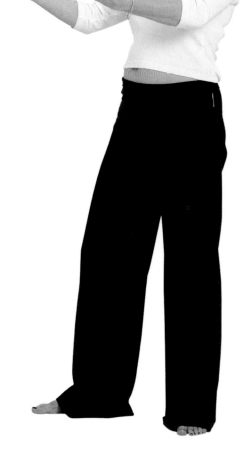

8 Make

up

They say that beauty is in the eye of the beholder. As far as we are concerned, the beholder needs to be blind or desperate to ever be attracted to our makeup-free faces. In the throes of our forties, we can no longer swish out the door with only a dab of moisturizer. Without makeup, we look like our faces have recently ploughed through a windshield…all lined, red, blotchy and cratered.

Susannah used to pity her older sister for never leaving home without foundation. She believed that would never be her, in spite of subjecting her skin to extreme weather conditions and years of smoking. The writing was always on the wall for Trinny. Having suffered acne, she is well versed in the merits of concealer and the art of facial disguise.

The irony is that while Susannah is the one blessed with good skin, Trinny is the one who always looks better on television and in photographs. Why? She is vain and very upfront about the fact. She LOVES makeup. She KNOWS how to apply the stuff and is on intimate terms with every new product. To say it is her obsession would be an understatement. So it is to her you must give the greatest nod of thanks for this chapter.

Susannah's contribution lies in recommending lazy ways with makeup for the girl who can't be bothered, has no time or hates the feeling of makeup on her skin. Thank Susannah for reducing the millions of products available down to the few we've highlighted in this chapter.

But the woman who has taught us the most, as well as telling us what to put in our makeup bags, has to be Charlotte Ribeyro. She has not only worked with us on our books and television series over the last few years but, more importantly, has also made us continuously aware of what we need to do.

The problem with makeup is that there are far too many choices. How on earth is a lay person supposed to wade through all those pigments, lipsticks, foundations, primers and preeners? What's the difference between cream and powder blush, oil-free and moisturizing foundation? Should you opt for a skin perfector or a skin brightener, a skin tint or a skin refiner? Which products should you look for to cover zits, to make the most of your eyes or keep your makeup fresh all day? We make these recommendations and also show in graphic detail some of the most common makeup mistakes.

To so many of us the language of makeup is as foreign as Swahili. Beautiful sounding, but incomprehensible. That is why women so often give in to freebies and magazine giveaways. They don't care that the color or the consistency of the product doesn't suit them; the fact that it is free takes away the fear of going into the cosmetics department and being sold something that they didn't want.

Makeup shopping is fraught with hazards. You might think you have hit the jackpot after reading a recommendation in a magazine. And, yes, that product probably is great and certainly looks so upon the fresh face of the 15-year-old model. Herein lies another peril. Once you've landed the brand of cosmetic, you need to know which products work for the age of your skin. For example, wrinkles should steer clear of powder, and pimples should give a wide berth to anything that will leave any sort of residue. During menopause your body goes through many physical changes, but the worst are hot flashes. You need to be sure that your makeup won't streak at these times.

The age issue is one we have paid great attention to in this chapter, separating products into groups that are best for specific times in our lives. The thing you will benefit most from, however, is the fact that we have sorted through the makeup product maze for you. Unobstructed by advertising budgets or other commitments, we have picked only those products that in our down-to-earth opinion actually do the business.

PREPARING YOUR SKIN

Some women's idea of preparing their skin for makeup is a bit of foundation or a dab of moisturizer; for others, it's a primer to keep foundation on and the skin oil-free.

Taking the time to prepare your skin with certain products will make your foundation go on more smoothly, ensure it lasts longer and give it a far better finish.

If your skin is not too sensitive, and you pile on the creams day in and day out, using a mask that takes away the buildup and dead skin cells will reveal a perfect pink glow to work with. Cleanse your face with Dr Sebagh's Deep Exfoliating Mask, followed with his Essential Glow and Crème Vital.

Beauty Flash Balm by Clarins can be used either as a mask thickly applied and then removed, or as a very thin layer that is left on, but it should not be rubbed too hard when the foundation is applied or bits come off on the skin. Rene Guinot's Masque Essentiel is great for a tired face, but remember to remove it with a hot facecloth as it is too thick to get off successfully with water and hands.

If you suffer from sallow smoker's skin that can look rather gray, try a skin illuminator like La Prairie's Rose Illusion Line Filler or Estée Lauder's Spotlight. They both contain ingredients which give a reflective light to the skin to counterbalance the dull appearance created by too many late nights, smoking or just general fatigue.

A foundation primer, such as NARS Makeup Primer, generally allows your foundation to go on more smoothly and will make it last longer, especially if it is a hot day. Primer is a relatively new invention – you'll notice the difference at one in the morning.

Top left to right NARS Makeup Primer, Origins A Perfect World White Tea Skin Guardian, Clarins Beauty Flash Balm. **Center** Guerlain Issima Midnight Star Extraordinary Radiance Treatment, Dr Sebagh Deep Exfoliating Mask, SK-11 Facial Treatment Essence. **Bottom** La Prairie Cellular Treatment Rose Illusion Line Filler, Estée Lauder Spotlight Skin Tone Perfector, Laura Mercier Secret Brightener.

BROWS

A woman's face is framed by her brows. We have come across so many women whose biggest beauty blunder has been a lack of respect to the grooming of these face-framers. Eyes can be opened up and the face entirely realigned by giving the brows a little tender loving care.

If you want to pluck your brows yourself, consider getting the set from Shavata. This renowned eyebrow expert has made up a fail-proof goody bag that includes the right shape brow you wish to achieve (an Elizabeth, a Kylie, etc.) that you stick on your existing brow so you can pluck around the area. It's a complete fallacy that you shouldn't pluck above the brow, probably invented by some worried mother who thought her daughter might pluck overzealously.

Some women prefer to put their brows in the hands of experts for threading, sugaring or waxing. If you do any of these, exfoliate for a week afterward to make sure you get no ingrown hairs with the regrowth. Most importantly, let the beautician know how much you want removed.

If your problem is more a lack of hair than subduing the forest, make sure you use a brush and eyebrow color in shadow form to fill in the cracks. There is nothing more unsightly (and aging) than a badly applied pencil line in a slightly off-ginger hue replacing the bald patch.

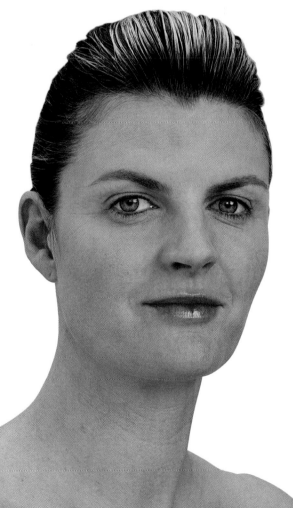

Tweezerman slant tweezers.
Left Susannah's untidy brow.
Right Carefully plucked, Susannah's brows now open up her face, even with no eye makeup.

SKIN

A flawless finish is what the bottle promises,
but if the product is badly applied the results
can be aging, blotchy and draining to the skin's
natural color. A well-applied base will ensure
that the rest of your makeup looks natural and
your skin glows.

When buying your foundation, don't get drawn
in by what it says on the bottle. Try it out on
your face, not your neck. (And why do people
insist on trying foundation on their wrist,
the palest part on the entire body?)
Take the makeup mirror
and go and check out the
color in the daylight to
get a realistic view of
the coverage as well
as the color.

Foundation should never be applied right under the eye to give thicker coverage; leave that work to the concealer. Always remember to smooth over and blend into the central part of your neck, which is generally paler than the rest of your face. A foundation's job is to even out the skin tone, and a concealer (that should be applied afterward) is used to focus on more obvious flaws.

Deciding which consistency of a foundation is right for you will depend on the quality and age of your skin.

Women in their 20s may still be suffering from hormonal spots or acne, so they should lean toward an oil-free foundation. Gel-based foundations are better for those who need less coverage, but just a gentle evening out of tone.

Some foundations carry their own built-in skin illuminators so you don't have to buy a separate product.

If you have worn the same foundation for 10 years, check that it still does the trick. It might be time to move on. In the last five years a huge number of innovative products have come on the market, so it's really worth making the rounds in your local department store.

From top to bottom Chantecaille Real Skin (a good foundation for young and older skin); Laura Mercier Moisturizing Foundation (gives good coverage for older skin); Barbara Daly for Tesco makeup (available in oil-free and moisturizing versions—something for all ages); Lancôme Transparence de Teint (good for the 20-30s age group); Prescriptives Traceless Skin Responsive Tint (suits skin of most ages).

CONCEALER

For women with great skin and only a few imperfections, a concealer might be all that is required for a flawless finish. A celebrated makeup artist we have worked with believes that too many women cover themselves with foundation when all they really need is some strategically placed concealer.

We are not suggesting that you go out and buy yet more products, but if you suffer from dark circles as well as zits, you might consider buying two different concealers – one for under the eyes and one for pimples. Alternatively, use just one (for around the eyes) and blend it in with some of your foundation. Do this by dabbing it on with your fingertips – blending is the key to successful application.

A universally loved product has got to be Touche Eclat by Yves Saint Laurent, but be careful when applying it that you do not create light rings around your eyes. Far better to use it together with another, slightly darker, concealer (Touche Eclat is rather chalky in color) and blend, blend, blend.

Cover-ups for scars and zits are thicker than those for around the eyes and need to be applied with a brush instead of the finger, which will take one dab to put on while the next will remove the coverage, ultimately leaving an unsightly buildup as you struggle to cover the offending area. Paula Dorf, Barbara Daly and Laura Mercier make great thin little brushes that do the trick.

When either of us have had a major zit outbreak, Benefit's Boi-ing and Laura Mercier's Secret Camouflage have saved us.

Top Susannah's scarring (left) is completely covered with the application of Dermacolor Camouflage Makeup Mini-Palette.
Middle Trinny's dark circles (left) are concealed with Yves St Laurent Touche Eclat, blended well with a little foundation.
Bottom Spots can be concealed with a product such as Laura Mercier's Secret Camouflage.

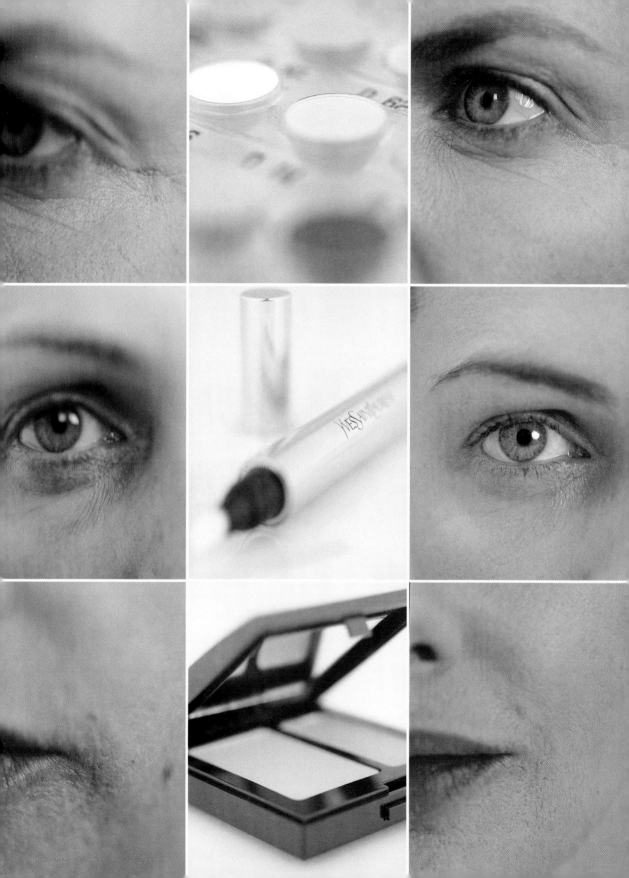

CHEEKS

Okay, the foundation is on, the spots are covered, and you no longer look like you need a week's rest to recover from your gallivanting lifestyle. Now, a lot of women will go straight to the eyes and lips or apply the bronzing powder.

Wait a minute. How would you like to capture that flush of heathy outdoor youth, the "I've just been fully satisfied in the bedroom" face? Well, blusher is your answer.

So many women get it so wrong that we feel the need to explain fully the benefits of avoiding the bronzer and going for the rosy cheeks look.

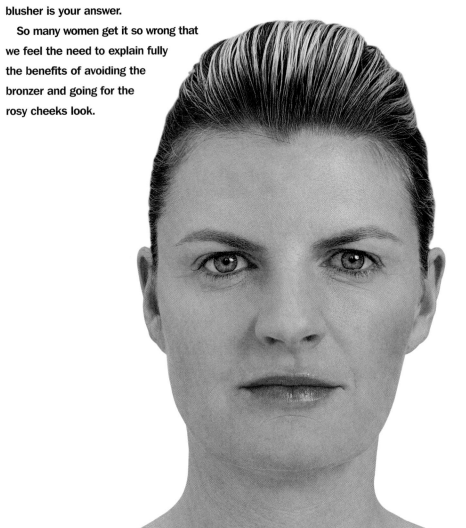

Much younger, chicer and less reminiscent of footballers' wives – we're sorry to categorize but they practically support the fake tan industry; blusher would be lost on their faces.

The key is to choose the blusher with the right color and texture to suit your skin.

If you are younger with a great peaches-and-cream complexion, go for an apricot powder blush. Make apples of your cheeks (by grinning inanely) and apply with a brush. Using powder as opposed to cream blusher will allow the look to stay at least until the end of dinner.

For a more mature complexion, where the cracks are beginning to show, cream blusher looks more natural, especially if you also have a slightly downy face.

Right Good for dry skins and hairy faces are Stila Convertible in Rose and NARS Multiple Stick.
Bottom right Good for oily skins and hair-free faces are RMK Powder Blush and Bourjois Powder Blush.

Susannah's face without blusher (the left hand side) and with blusher (right), showing how the color gives structure and rosiness to her face.

LIPS

The number of unsuccessfully enhanced lips about only goes to show how many people are dissatisfied with the way they look. But you don't always have to resort to cosmetic surgery to remedy an unattractive pout.

As you get older, the appearance of lines above the mouth (particularly if you've ever been a smoker) can be one of the least attractive aspects of aging. It is possible to diminish this problem.

Rubbing night cream vigorously into your lips will help, but it is the fillers that go under your lipstick that make the most difference. Both The Body Shop's wax filler and Guerlain's Lip Lift fill in the lines sufficiently so that when covered with a lip gloss (avoid lipstick as it will run) the look is far smoother.

Thin lips can be a sign of meanness, but why let on when you can boost your natural pout with a bit of DuWop's Lip Venom? The cinnamon ingredients react against the skin and puff up the lip area. For best results, apply often.

To remedy a crooked mouth, a very careful application of the right-colored lip liner (we love MAC's lip pencil in Spice) should reduce the difference in size. Just be careful to blend liner well to avoid the drag queen lip liner look.

From top to bottom The product, and before and after: Guerlain Divinora Lip Lift will help to fill out lines. DuWop Lip Venom plumps up your pout. MAC Spice Lip Pencil helps even out the contours of your mouth.

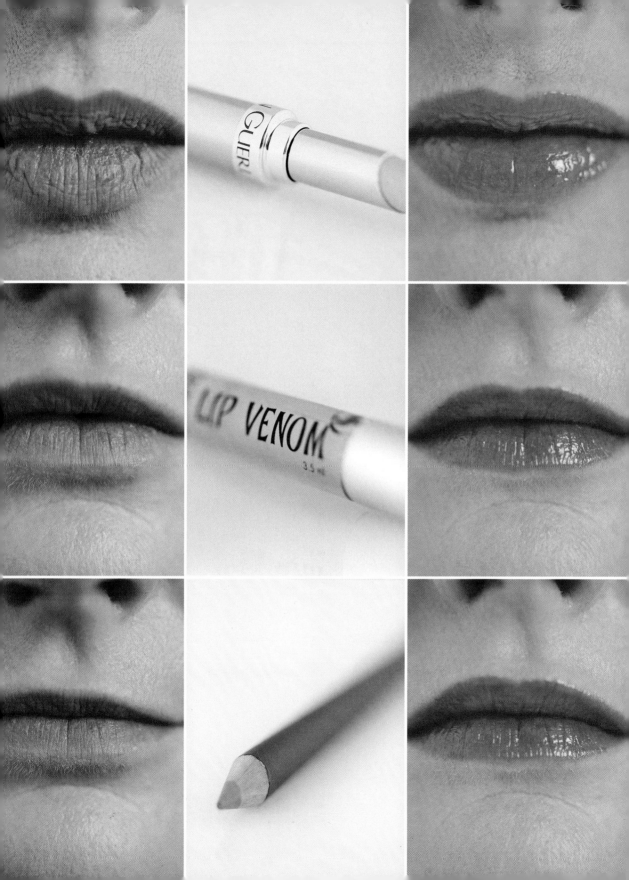

EYES

The most commonly asked questions we get are: "How do I apply eye-shadow?", "How do I get rid of that greasy line that develops in my eye socket a couple of hours after I've applied my makeup?" and "What's the best mascara?"

These questions are from women who have been making up their faces for years. The trouble is that we get into a routine and it sticks. Our eyelids might droop, our hair color might change and the wrinkles get deeper, but still we put on that heavy black kohl for the panda eyes look.

Well, it's time for a wake-up call. Sit down in front of the mirror with good natural light and look honestly at the windows to your soul. What do you see?

If your eyes are hooded, you need to use products that open up the area and enlarge the eye (which is probably getting lost among the folds). Brighten your entire undereye area with YSL Touche Eclat, use smoky eye shadow to put a thickly smudged line on your top lid and curl your eyelashes; for extra impact at nighttime, line the inner bottom ring of your eye.

If your eyes are deep set, use the flesh-colored NARS Blonde Eye Shadow liberally over your lid, curl your eyelashes with a heated lash wand and apply a generous amount of mascara; for more drama, use Maybelline Cool Effects eye shadow in your socket to define your eyelid further. The main thing to remember for deep-set eyes is to keep sparkly eyeshadow to a

minimum because it will only make the rest of your eye recede even further.

If you suffer from bad lines around your eyes, apply Prescriptives Invisible Lines Smoother to the crow's-feet, then use Laura Mercier Eye Basic over the lid. This will give color, but won't enhance the lines.

Try to steer clear of any powder products. If you want a bit of sparkle, try something such as Revlon Eyeglide Shimmer Shadow, but keep it close to the lash line. Curl your eyelashes and use mascara.

For hooded eyes Shu Uemura Eyelash Curler, YSL False Lash Effect Mascara, NARS Eyeliner Pencil, Bourjois Eyeshadow in Gris Magnetique and Eylure Individual Lashes.
For deepset eyes Estée Lauder MagnoScopic Mascara, ModelCo Lash Wand Heated Eyelash Curler, Maybelline Cool Effect Shadow/Liner Pencil and NARS Blonde Eye Shadow.
For lined eyes Tesco Eyelash Curler, Magic by Prescriptives Invisible Line Smoother, Laura Mercier Eye Basics, Revlon Eyeglide Shimmer Shadow and Maybelline Great Lash Mascara.

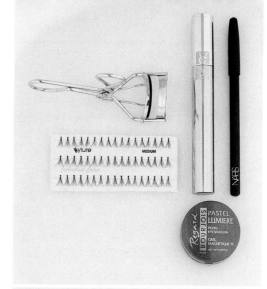

NAILS

Your makeup is exquisitely applied, every hair on your head is glossy and shining…but look down at your nails. Are they chipped, bitten and dirty? No woman can really look her best if her nails are a mess. You don't have to cultivate long red talons – leave those to the beauty queens for scratching each other's eyes out. Just clean, neatly shaped nails with a gleam of flattering, even clear, nail polish. And if you have nails that tend to break and flake, the polish actually does help to protect them.

The easiest way to keep your nails looking good is to go for regular manicures – and pedicures – but it's perfectly simple to DIY. Obviously you'll start by making sure your nails are sparkling clean and not looking like you've just dug potatoes with your bare hands. We all know not to use metal files, but did you know you can get glass nail files? These give a finer, gentler result and you can file in both directions. Otherwise use padded emery boards rather than the old-fashioned sandpaper types. Before applying polish, wipe your nails over with nail polish remover to get rid of any grime or grease – helps the polish go on better, too. Always put on a base coat and top coat as well as your color polish. Reapply the top coat every couple of days to help it last.

Simpler still, polish your nails with a buffer that gives them a natural shine.

Oh my...

"A woman's first job is to choose the right shade of lipstick "

Carole Lombard

Some women don't even suit lipstick. Don't always think it's the one product that will "cheer up" your face.

S

HOW TO KEEP YOUR MAKEUP FRESH ALL DAY

Many a woman's answer to this is never to give it a chance to wear off in the first place. Long-lasting lipsticks that dry out, constant foundation plastering and powder overload – these don't make an attractive image. Far better to invest in some great products to freshen you and keep you on top of the situation.

A fab makeup primer will guarantee your makeup and foundation will last and stay looking smooth and airbrushed. In the afternoon when things start to look a little tired (perhaps), don't add more; simply work some Rosebud Salve into your fingertips and pat around the areas that need perking up and voilà, your base and face will regain its peachy glow.

Don't pile on the powder – it looks cakey and it's messy to carry around. Use blotting sheets to remove excess oil without product overload. Benefit's Dr. Feelgood does the same trick and works well under or over your foundation.

Long-lasting lipstick is a crime. It does not look attractive to have a dried-on crust. Use normal products and if it's the aging feathering that concerns you, prepare your lips with a waxy line filler like Body Shop Lip Line Fixer or Paula Dorf Perfect Illusion to make sure your lipstick stays where it ought to. Lipstick was not meant to last all day and the new natural, feather-light products are designed to be reapplied.

Eye-shadow debris? Lipline error? Simply whip out a ModelCo makeup remover bud and wipe away any mishap without the paraphernalia of cleanse, tone, and moisturize. To refresh your face without splashing it with cold water, use a mineral mist that also fixes your makeup.

We love Crème de la Mer The Mist.

If you are having a long day at the office, followed by a night of excess, start the day with a good eye brightener applied under the eyes and in the corners of your nose. Benefit Ooh La Lift, Laura Mercier Secret Brightener and Guerlain Happology Eye Cream work wonders.

Above Stila mini brush set.
Top left to right Benefit Ooh La Lift, Laura Mercier Secret Finish, Body Shop Lip Line Fixer.
Centre Barbara's Private Collection Mineral Mist, Benefit Dr. Feelgood Invisible Refiner, ModelCo Makeup Remover Cotton Buds.
Below Crème de la Mer The Mist, Smith's Rosebud Salve, Clinique Stay-Matte Oil Blotting Sheets.

This is the runway of cheek color that whizzes down the cheek bone, a prerequisite for the inexperienced. Teenage girls, especially, often wear blusher that looks as if it has been applied by a painter and decorator. Many see the errors of their ways eventually, but many more don't, and are left looking dated and unsophisticated.

Those afflicted with the Roman road blusher look usually make the mistake of using the brush that comes with the blush. These are invariably too small and blunt-ended, making it impossible to get a soft coverage.

Using a color that isn't suited to your natural skin tone also turns your blusher into an embarrassment. Blush is sold to enhance your coloring and make you look healthy and well. It is there to give definition to your cheek bones and NOT to define your whole face. Using a mismatched pigment is overpowering and theatrical. The end result must be less like Coco the Clown and more like Coco Chanel.

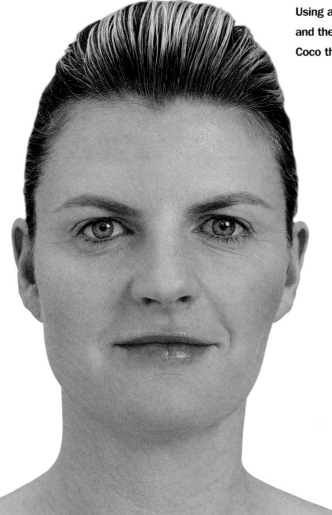

We see a lot of this. So many women literally lacquer their lashes with layer upon layer of mascara. Why, we ask ourselves, do they do this? Of course the eyes are the mirror to the soul, but how the hell are you supposed to look in when they are curtained by thick, black, hairy spiders' legs?

The eyes are the most important feature of one's face. In surveys that ask men what physical attributes attract them to a woman, it's the eyes that come way up there...well, after tits, legs and butt. "Oh, doesn't she have beautiful eyes," is a line used when there isn't much else to compliment. "It's in the eyes" is a phrase used to underline behavioral characteristics. Is it for these reasons that so much time goes into overapplying mascara?

Lots of women say they feel naked without mascara. This isn't surprising because thick lashes go a long way toward enhancing the eyes. What doesn't help is the addition of lumpy clumps that hang precariously from lashes, like skin tags you long to pull off.

We agree that at least two applications of mascara is a good idea, but they must be clog-free. Wouldn't you rather have lashes that look naturally thick and glossy as opposed to resembling lumpy gravy?

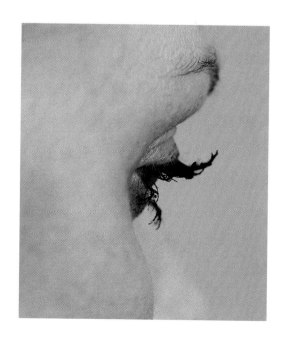

Made-up lips should look natural. As soon as you start drawing an outline with a lip pencil it looks…well, drawn in. Regardless of the fact that so many of you do it, there is no earthly reason why a fake pout should be more appealing than the real thing. The whole point of makeup is that it should either look as natural as Elizabeth Arden will allow, or when piled on for a party, should be blended as if applied by a neoclassical painter.

The thing about lip liner is that no matter how flawlessly it is drawn on it will still look tacky. If your lips are enclosed by a fence of dark pencil, they will look tiny, pinched and mean because you will have cut right into their fullness.

We think lip liners have a purpose, but one that is limited to dark lipsticks that need to be applied to the lips with great precision. Even in this instance, the pencil should be of exactly the same color as the lipstick, otherwise no matter how clever you are, you will still muck it up.

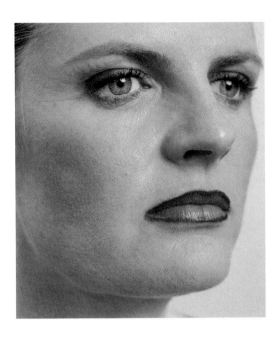

There is no point in achieving flawless skin with makeup if the foundation you are wearing doesn't match your skin tone. You might have a perfectly smooth shade of tawny on your face, but if this color doesn't carry down over the jaw and onto your neck, the effect is disastrous. A tidemark of foundation along the jaw makes you look like you haven't had a bath in weeks and if you are prone to breakouts, the swampy, sticky residue is a perfect breeding ground for those spots.

In the same way that we forget to look at our rear view before leaving the house, whether through fear or genuine absentmindedness, we forget that our neck is attached to our face.

Makeup can be like a mask, an illusion to give confidence, but it should be a disguise that only you are aware of. Show the world that your beauty was bought in a bottle, and you are suddenly less attractive.

The trick is getting one of the girls behind the makeup counter to help you match your foundation exactly to your skin. She should apply a smudge on your jaw line and if you can't see it, you have a good match. This will in turn make application so much easier and leave no room for dirty streaks.

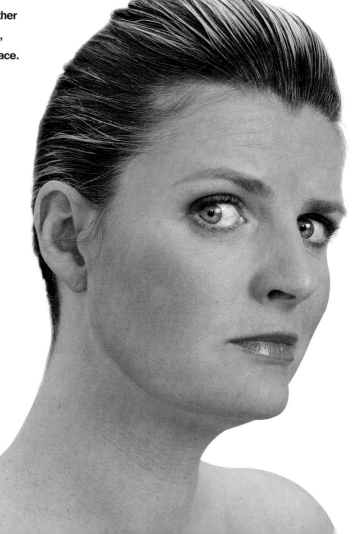

CLASSIC MISTAKES EYEBROWS

Another instance where less is more. Eyebrows frame the face, and correcting brow imperfections can change a woman's appearance quite dramatically.

Too pale a brow leaves a face bland and devoid of definition, but too hard a line turns a girl into Groucho Marx.

Painting the brow in with a hard pencil also leaves the brow looking as if it has been stuck on like a false moustache.

Look at the Elizabeths Hurley and Taylor to see how attractive a beautifully arched brow can be.

CLASSIC MISTAKES BRONZER

It is lovely to feel healthy and well. It is almost more satisfying to *look* healthy and well. Blusher does this superbly, even on pale skins. Women who believe healthy living comes from a compact of bronzing powder or fake tan are absolutely right...if it's a Jaffa orange they are wanting to emulate.

A heavy hand armed with a bronzing brush gives the face the unreal aura of having been to the bronzing pot as opposed to the sun. An over-bronzed face becomes a façade that must be hiding a multitude of sins in a very unsubtle manner.

Leave your skin color as nature intended. If you want a tan, get it in very small doses from the rays, rather than from crushed terracotta straight out of the potting shed.

EMERGENCY

An emergency situation calls for drastic action. You've had a week of late nights already, but it's your best friend's wedding – you have to go! You look in the mirror and think to yourself, "What beauty product can possibly save me?" As much as the product itself, your salvation lies in the skill with which you apply it.

The first thing you need to do is to give your face an invigorating massage. Start by pressing firmly with your fingertips from the center of your forehead out to, and along, your hairline.

Next, for a really rosy-cheeked moment, put your thumb in your mouth, pushing it as high up as possible inside your cheek cavity, then with your second and third fingers on the outside of your cheek, pull the the skin away from your mouth and across to your ear, really pressing the cheekbone quite firmly. Do it two or three times. Watch the rosy glow return to your face. It is advisable when practicing this "instant face-lift" to have short thumbnails.

After all this your face should have really woken up. For the final stimulation, take a good facial scrub (we love Korner's exfoliator or Jason Vita-C Max) and spend five minutes massaging it into your face. Then remove it with a really hot facecloth. Rinse the facecloth out and then sploosh your face again, this time with really cold water.

You are now ready to apply some of the products in Preparing Your Skin on pages 186-187.

Help!!!

$

Drink loads of water. Give your skin a really good massage to bring the circulation back and remove dryness. Put a couple of cucumber slices on your eyes.

$$

Aveda Intensive Hydrating Masque

Darphin Instant Radiance Vitaserum

Elizabeth Arden Peel & Reveal

Estee Lauder Idealist Micro-D Deep Thermal Refinisher

The Organic Pharmacy Collagen Boost Antioxidant Gel Mask

Origins Out of Trouble 10 Minute Mask

Eve Lom Dynaspot

Jason Vita-C Max One Minute Facial

Origins Never A Dull Moment

$$$

Chantecaille Jasmine and Lily Healing Mask

Talika Eye Therapy Patch

Rodial Glam Balm

Crème de La Mer The Refining Facial

Jan Marini Clean Zyme Green Papaya Skin Cleanser

Jan Marini Skin Zyme Papaya Mask

Thalgo Youthful Look Patch Mask

Dr Sebagh Deep Exfoliating Mask, Essential Glow and Crème Vital

Dr Sebagh Serum Repair

Prescriptives Dermapolish System

Caudalie Vinotherapie Eye Lifting Serum

Eve Lom Rescue Mask

The Lift Petite facial mask

Korner the Exfoliator

Clockwise from top Jason Vita-C Max One Minute Facial, Eve Lom Rescue Mask, Jan Marini Clean Zyme Green Papaya Skin Cleanser, Jan Marini Skin Zyme Green Papaya Mask, Thalgo Youthful Look Patch Mask and Dr Sebagh Serum Repair.

"The older you are, the less makeup you should look like you are wearing, even though it might take you longer to apply. If you've worn the same makeup for the last five years, it's time to re-evaluate."

S

9
Travel

Having a good holiday lies in the preparation, and a happy return depends on how good you look in the holiday photos. It matters not one iota that you are bound for the Barrier Reef if you have packed all the wrong things. Your homecoming, tanned and rested, will be unusually anticlimactic if you look like a pig in all the photographs. This may sound shallow and superficial to men and the naturally poised, but they haven't gone through the trauma of Bikini-Top-Left-Behinditis or always being caught at the wrong angle by a camera. To girls still stalked by baby fat and us women plummeting into middle age and beyond, the science of packing and posing is a subject that should be learned.

We do appreciate that there are a few to whom packing means two thongs, a toothbrush and malaria tablets. These are dropouts or eternal students on a quest for a spiritual wake-up call so don't pay any attention to them or use their Barbie-sized backpacks as a yardstick by which to measure your trunk. Yes, it is nice to travel light, but that takes years of experience or an up-the-world attitude exclusive to the aforementioned dropouts or the physically perfect. The bulk of us want to look our best, without standing out as the tourists that we are. Having the correct clothing can really make or break a holiday.

There's nothing worse than going to a country and not bringing your favorite products because you didn't think there was room in your suitcase. Collecting samples of products you already use is better than taking the free samples of something you will never try. And take the time a few days before you go to decant your favorite beauty products into travel-sized containers.

One could say that Trinny was a gifted packer, in the sense that she can turn around two weeks' worth of clothes and pop them in however many suitcases it takes the night before departure. She has an eye for what's required and can glance through her wardrobes to select probably too much but everything she could possibly need, including an empty bag to carry all the stuff she'll buy once on vacation. She'll want for nothing and will live in a microcosm of the perfectly groomed. Susannah can attain the same results but hers is a more cultured method that requires a great deal of time and forethought. She likes to travel with the minimum. This means working out every outfit for every day prior to packing, and assuming that all countries are third world and unable to provide toothpaste, Tampax, shampoo, hairdryers, sun lotion, etc. Although she doesn't have the "just-in-case" attitude, her suitcase will probably be the same size as Trinny's because in terms of sundries (anything other than clothes), she will have it all... including film and batteries for the camera.

The camera can be the most dangerous beast that you encounter in foreign climates. It can kill all sense of decorum and shatter self-confidence just by poking its lens up your skirt, down your cleavage or deep into the folds of your stomach. Never, and we mean never, allow yourself to be too laid-back about having your picture taken. The lens is your enemy and has to be attacked with enormous amounts of posing done in a way that looks completely natural. When you are not perfect you cannot leave your photo appearance to chance...strike a pose and wear your favorite holiday clothes to be sure of having glamorous, not grungy, memories of your precious free time.

Now, the journey itself. When you travel with small children and babies you have to think about practicality as well as comfort and style. When you're stuck on a plane for hours on end close to sticky fingers and flying drinks you don't want to have to worry about your velvet jacket or suede skirt. Think sensibly and wear colors that won't show dirt and grime, and fabrics that can be chucked in a washing machine as soon as you arrive – looking like the chocolate mousse served for your airline meal.

MINIMIZING YOUR TOILETRIES

The clothes are packed, you close the suitcase, test the weight, and oh, by Jove, it's really not that heavy. Wow, how fab. You might even be able to sneak it on as hand luggage. And then you put in your toiletries bag, followed by sun lotion, shampoo and beach bag. Next comes the makeup, which you implant carefully down the side where there is a small space between your underwear and flip-flops. You squeeze the case closed and perform another lift test. Your arm is pulled from its socket. You spend the two-week vacation strapped up with a shoulder dislocation.

It's always the toiletries that bugger up your carefully laid packing plans. They weigh more than anything else, invariably leak and

are usually left behind half full at the end of your holiday because you can't be bothered to carry them back home.

Have you ever heard of miniature sizes or the method of decanting beauty stuff into lightweight plastic containers?

Let us introduce you to the joys of less-is-more-room for sexy tops and sundresses. The collation of miniature products doesn't happen overnight. It can be hard to find what you need in small form. You have to keep your eyes peeled at every pharmacist, supermarket and beauty counter for mini versions of your favorite cosmetics. If they are not on display, ask for them and never turn down a free sample, however annoying the woman handing them out might be.

Fortunately, cosmetic companies have begun to meet the demand for travel sizes. You can get pretty much everything from shampoo to toothpaste and even body scrubs in teeny bottles or sachets. The beauty of baby-sized products is that they are lighter, take up less room and avoid wastage.

Above These are the products we pack in our toiletries bags. Brands we like are shown here, but you will have your own favorite versions.

Top row body lotion, bath oil, lip gloss, foundation.

Middle row shampoo, conditioner, skin tonic, body mist, tinted moisturizer, day cream, cleanser.

Bottom row toothpaste, deodorant, hair styling lotion, after-sun cream, sun screen.

Right Most of the above come in mini versions or sample sizes. Those that don't, we decant into little bottles and jars from Muji.

HOW TO PACK A SUITCASE

Amazingly, it is Susannah who has perfected the art of packing a suitcase. Not the actual physical packing of the clothes (that she learned from Trinny), but the ability to take only what she needs and get it into a hold-all small enough to slide into the overhead compartments on a plane. This miraculous feat was born from a desire to always avoid checking her luggage. Waiting at the carousel while baggage handlers idle back from lunch or are on strike became a nightmare, when all Suz wanted to do was get back to her family as quickly as possible.

Small-time packing is much easier, and to be honest only truly possible, in the summer. The light fabrics fold into nothing. Coats and jackets are unnecessary and one's footwear is much less clumpy.

When traveling to a colder climate, the trick is to wear all the bulky stuff, like warm coat and boots, on the flight. The boots should be smart enough for business and flat enough to wear day in, day out. These need to be accompanied by one pair of heels for the evenings.

When it comes to the actual filling of your suitcase you must rid yourself of the stereotypical method of putting the heavy stuff at the bottom so that it doesn't squash your clothes. The best way is the reverse. If you put all the hardware on top, it acts as a press and keeps the clothes beneath unable to wriggle around and get creased. It also means there are more nooks and crannies in which to stuff last-minute bits and pieces.

Lots of small items and clothes folded flat or into tiny bundles are more packing-friendly than one big down coat or jumbo cord trousers.

Top Put heavy items on top to keep everything else in place.
Center Place folded items, such as tops and jackets, in the middle layer.
Bottom Start by placing the items that you want to remain flat, such as trousers and skirts.

WHAT TO CARRY LONG HAUL

There is no getting away from the fact that long-haul flights are completely awful. Twelve hours of compressed air filled with other people's germs and a seat that turns buttocks into hard, overcooked minced beef makes you wonder whether two weeks on a beach is worth the agony of the flight. This is a natural attitude but one that you have to get over. If you think of your airplane seat as a bedroom and equip it accordingly, the journey will be much improved.

A cabin-sized bag can carry everything you need on the flight as well as reading matter. These are our essentials. **Top row opposite** pashmina (folds into nothing and is warmer and less smelly than an airline blanket), eye mask, toothbrush and toothpaste, cashmere socks (warm and won't make your feet sweat).

Think of the essentials you need for a good night's sleep. If it's a pill, take one. If it's a soft pillow, take that, too. If your feet tend to get chilled, bring warm socks on board, and if you are germ-phobic, spray your space with tea-tree oil.

Prepare yourself as you would at bedtime. This ritual will help you relax and make you feel at home. Take off your makeup, brush your teeth. Have a hot drink, then take a pee. Be comfortable in your clothes or even change into pajama-type bottoms. You will look totally mad doing all these things, and you won't be picked up by a handsome stranger while you have wax in your ears, an eye mask and a dribbling chin from the deep sleep your pre-flight planning has promoted. But you will arrive refreshed.

Center row below compact with a little mirror, Jurlique Rosewater Skin Freshener (wonderfully refreshing), Stress Mints (homeopathic stress remedies in mint form), Guerlain Midnight Secret (the best, but most expensive, flight hydration cream), washcloth, ear plugs.

Bottom row neck pillow, mouthwash, homeopathic jet lag remedy, eye drops, Dornomyl (herbal sleep aid), Organic Pharmacy herbal in-flight spray, Rescue Remedy (for those scary bumpy moments, spray vitamins (easy to absorb and gentler on the stomach than tablets), Evian water.

"Modern traveling is
it is merely being
and very little
becoming a

not traveling at all;
sent to a place,
different from
parcel **"**

John Ruskin

f you are a parcel,
at least be well wrapped. **⊤s**

Most people feel stupid posing for a photo. It's hardly surprising when you see the results – chins descending into cleavage, legs looking six inches long, stomach settling into rolls. It takes guts to go for the pose that flatters your body to its best advantage because posing gives away the fact that you feel less than perfect. But, while it is embarrassing the first few times, it becomes second nature. Soon you will always look your best, and what bliss to have the advantage over those who are younger, thinner and prettier than you simply by being stunningly photogenic and a gift to all amateur snappers.

BIG BOOBS

Big boobs can very quickly turn to fat unless they are manipulated into shape with good posture. You must never lean forward to bunch them together as this looks cheap and too porn star (if you are young) or barmaid (if you are old, like Susannah here). What you must do is thrust them out by keeping your shoulders back.

We don't mean an arched tabloid thrust but one that is more relaxed, a stance that is achieved by keeping the arms limp. If the boobs are held forward they don't merge into any fat folds elsewhere.

NO BOOBS

The last thing you want to look like in your holiday photos is a man in drag. You don't want your bikini top to look pointless, with the two triangles empty of anything to grasp hold of. If you do get caught by a roving camera lens while lying on your back, your boobs (what there is of them) will disappear under your arms and look like pectorals instead of breasts. You'll look like a bodybuilder as opposed to a glamorous beach babe. Sit up, for goodness sake. Keep your back straight and arms away from your sides so that your little mounds don't become part of your arms. Easy to do and you'll be amazed at the results.

SHORT LEGS

If you don't like your legs you may have a tendency to try to tuck them away underneath the chair or whatever you may be sitting on – anything to keep them away from a prying camera. Unfortunately your embarrassment is doing your legs no favors. They'll look a foot shorter if the only part you can see is your calves. You can so easily extend the leg by showing more flesh. Part them and camouflage with a casual hand or dangling hat. It's really that newborn foal or Bambi stance that we're after. One where your pins have the look of being too thin to carry your torso.

BIG ARMS

We do believe that these should be covered whenever possible, but there are occasions when this is just not an option. On the beach is that time. To suddenly reach for a sarong to cover them would be too much and not possible anyway with something in your hand. And it's the something in your hand that is the essential ingredient for a thinner limb. If you are carrying sunglasses, a hat or a drink, it looks more natural to have the free mitt casually placed upon your hip. Keeping some distance between the arm and your body leaves room for fat to dangle down out of the way.

NO WAIST

This is a no-brainer. Simply use your hands as a corset to winch in that non-existent curve. Your action will automatically make you stand better and create a dent in the sides of your torso.

SADDLEBAGS

Disguising this problem is a little more contrived because it means asking the photographer to move positions and take the picture from behind. You, in turn, have to distort your neck, providing a clear view of your face for the camera. Taking a picture from this angle elongates the legs. Just don't forget to lift your thighs away from the sun lounger so that, as with fat arms, the superfluous flesh hangs down and stays well out of sight.

FLABBY TUMMY

There is no real trick to ridding yourself temporarily of a big tum. You can't suck it away, and turning your back to the camera (the only cast-iron method of being rid of a tummy) is, well, pointless. You can, of course, sling something over it, but that becomes too obvious after the tenth picture of you with a towel draped over your middle. The best suggestion we can offer (and we admit it's not fail-safe) is to lie flat, suck in and hold your breath with a big smile that defies the agony you're going through to pull that pose.

NO NECK

If your neck is less than swanlike, an unwary snap can leave you looking like your head comes straight from your shoulders.

The solution below is a balance between getting the neck to appear longer without the lens heading straight up your nose, which can make the loveliest of us look uncannily equine.

When the camera threatens, take a moment to strike a reasonable pose – you'll thank us for this later. Lie with your head tilted back slightly and your chin up and you will be surprised how elegant your neck will look. Make sure you are still below the level of photographer and camera to avoid horsey nostrils.

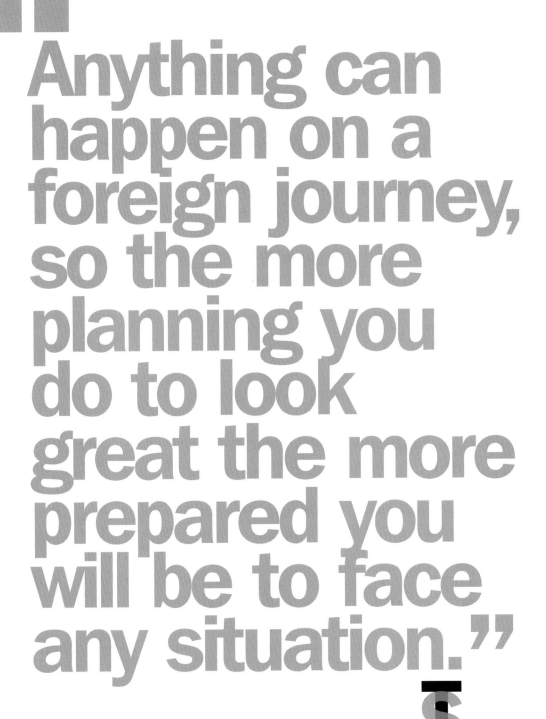

"Anything can happen on a foreign journey, so the more planning you do to look great the more prepared you will be to face any situation."

10
Pregn

There is no getting away from the fact that being pregnant takes a while to get used to. Feet become a figment of some distant past when you were able to see them. Sleeping silently on one's back is replaced by lying in a fortress of pillows and snoring loudly enough to awaken the neighbors and yourself.

Although we've been lucky in all our collective pregnancies in terms of health, our happiness was thwarted slightly by feelings of hurtling through something resembling a midlife crisis.

We can make most tummies disappear, but there are limits...pregnant stomachs being one. The thing is, with protruding bellies, there is no getting away from the fact that we were not up for grabs. It's not like you can pretend to be young, free and possibly single. This means any thoughts of flirting with boys young enough to be "nephews" need to be shelved. Even as the proverbial "older woman," we are not an option when we look and feel very much like wet sandbags.

Tiresome though this temporary confinement on our sexuality was, we found other ways to amuse ourselves. The first and most enjoyable was simply to give in to food. The second was finding ways to look decent enough for our husbands, who are funnier and better looking than any tiresome youths, to continue to fancy us. Ironically, the latter was easier for Susannah because her obsession with clothes is not a life or death condition. Imagine how hard it was for Trinny, to whom fat is an alien nation and fashion her heart's blood, watching her skinny frame bursting the seams of immaculate outfits.

Pregnancy highlights and expands what you hate about your body. Having tits and tum as problem areas anyway made pregnant life smoother for Susannah, because these are the areas that get bigger naturally when having a baby (in case any woman hasn't noticed!). Adapting her look was simply a question of extending her existing garments. Trinny, on the other hand, had to cope with elephantine legs, broadening hips *and* a swelling tummy and tits, a fact that really did her head in for a while.

In spite of clothes getting tighter, our resolve never to touch maternity wear remained unbroken. We once walked into one of those shops where the mannequins have balloonlike growths and vowed never to return.

Why would any woman with child want to make herself look not just like a tent, but the whole camp? The real turnoff was those trousers with the specifically engineered panels. Once we were both four months into gestation, our irregular shapes forced us toward pregnancy jeans. All we can say is that Earl Jeans had the last laugh on Susannah as she lived in the two pairs bought with excited relief, while Trinny, ever the true style guru, got her trousers specially fitted by a handy dressmaker.

Anyone who's had a baby will know that one remains pregnant for a few weeks after giving birth, so don't assume you can pack away the clothes you wore while you were pregnant; they will stand you in good stead afterward. This is depressing, but there is no point in buying anything new for at least three months postbirth. If you need retail therapy, which you invariably will, especially after looking at yourself naked in front of a full-length mirror, splash out on clothes for your baby or buy really expensive accessories for yourself.

Once you have had the baby, and if you are breastfeeding, your breasts will leak, so avoid anything too pale that will show moisture like sweat marks under your arms. And don't wear anything that's too tight around the waist.

Pregnancy is a tough one to combat in all respects, but if you look good then, everything in life becomes so much more pleasurable. It was a challenge for us, but one we thoroughly enjoyed.

WINTER CASUAL WEAR

It is so easy to slide into the murky world of husband's shirts and comfy leggings when pregnant. Nobody, however marvelous, beautiful, perfect and thin they are, looks dignified submerged in a baggy button down and saggy-arsed, footless tights. This combination is offensively awful and an injustice to the beauty of the pregnant form. If your legs remain skinny, and more importantly, your butt doesn't get too huge, show them off in tightish trousers and your bump in a skinny top. At least then you will look pregnant as opposed to deformed.

Have you ever seen Trinny look as ghastly as she does in this jumpsuit? The fact that she can stand there with a straight face is in itself quite remarkable. Her arse, already not her best feature, is blown out of all proportion when encased in padded nylon. She needs to show her bump in relaxed, fitted, lightweight wool, with cozy wide-leg pants that envelop her ever-increasing, childbearing hips.

you've got to be joking!

WINTER WORK WEAR

Susannah loves the idea of a dress over trousers. What a shame then that she looks so vile in this useful and stylish clothing concept. Why? Well, the dress tents her stomach, hiding the skinniest part of her big form – her hips and bum. This is the very reason the tight figure-hugging dress works so well. It proudly displays that her stomach is so huge there could be a whole litter nestling within its vastness.

Poor Trinny's legs suffered terribly during pregnancy. Words like swollen, elephantine, and city-servicing water-tank retention can be accurately used to describe her lower half in this skirt. You would not think they were the same legs in this comely long jacket that hides it all. The heels add length to her stumps, which in these long trousers look lithe and elegant…no mean achievement.

WINTER EVENING WEAR

Susannah looks like she could hide a three-seater sofa up her skirt. Do look at how enormous this billowing chiffon makes her appear. This may be one fancy skirt she can get into, but so could all the other guests... at the same time. A pregnant stomach enveloped in a small print has its size diffused, while the legs can continue to carry off jeans, albeit pregnancy ones.

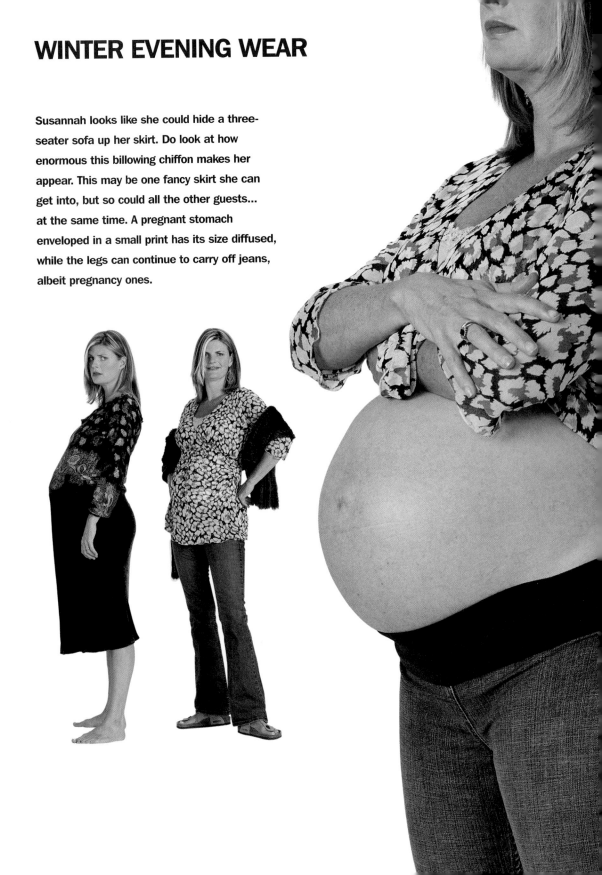

Even when pregnant, Trinny just cannot afford to wear a dress so tight that it shows where her bum ends and short stumpy legs begin – in fact, pregnancy makes it worse. But she *can* wear a dress over trousers. As when not pregnant, she still needs to try to shorten her back and lengthen her legs, which this outfit does by neatly disguising her bottom.

WINTER PARTY WEAR

Pregnancy is the only time Susannah's fat arms are allowed on show and that's because they look relatively small beside her enormous breasts. She cannot, however, be seen dead in a strappy little number, because the smallness of the dress makes her huge frame look even larger. Much better for Suz to keep things long, tight and streamlined.

You have got to give it to her – the girl is
brave to be photographed in these salami-leg-
turning tights and this sausagelike, skintight
dress. Trinny would look great in the window
of a butcher's shop, but not at a film premiere.
For her, the dress-over-trouser theme continues
to work beautifully for camouflaging her bottom
and legs.

"I didn't have to buy any new outfits when I was pregnant; I just went to my husband's wardrobe"

Anonymous

**I wonder how long
that marriage lasted.**

SUMMER CASUAL WEAR

Many young mothers-to-be adopt the "let it all hang out" approach. Not us. We are too old and too square for that. It is hard to be casual and cool while keeping comfortable and looking relaxed. That's why Susannah lives in sarongs during summer pregnancies (she sounds like a brood mare). They can be tied to fit precisely and they look great with a fun T-shirt and flat gold or silver flip-flops or Birkenstocks.

As soon as Trinny does a floaty skirt or dress without the trousers she looks like she might take off. For her thickening ankles, trousers were the only option, and as her arms remained unaffected by baby, she was able to show them off in simple vests. A nice clean outfit like this is a great solution for those wanting comfort and practicality.

SUMMER WORK WEAR

It's not easy to look smart at work while remaining cool. Susannah found the ideal solution in tight-fitting dresses with cardigans. Tempted toward crisp cotton skirts, she was soon put off by the fact she resembled a pot-bellied pig dressed in human clothes. Fabrics with a bit of stretch have the bonus of remaining crease free.

When it's hot and you are with child, the appeal of pretty summer dresses is irresistible. You think of the lovely draughtiness they provide and the earth-motherliness they represent. But they can sadly damage your reputation at work because, being voluminous, they billow like sails over the bump. If you carry your weight down below and want to be pretty yet professional, wrap your belly in flowers and, as ever, stick the pack atop a pair of casually fitting trousers.

not from here honey!

SUMMER EVENING WEAR

Oh, it's so lovely to go ethnic in the summer,
but you have to choose your country of influence
cleverly when shaped like Susannah. As she
so clearly demonstrates, big-tented tops make
her look frumpy and ready for the forceps.
A slim-line kaftan, belted under the bump,
looks relaxed, fun and much more flattering.

As soon as that butt goes on display it all starts to go horribly wrong. The combination of tight top and trousers shows that Trinny's bottom is as big as the baby-carrying tummy. Yet again, the dress-over-trousers look, and one that shows off her temporarily large breasts, is boosting both emotionally and physically.

SUMMER PARTY WEAR

Never be lured into thinking that flowers and froth work if your boobs are as big as your belly. Even at normal, lactating-free moments, big prints do nothing for large breasts other than make your assets look bloated. Think back to the everyday rules of boob dressing and keep the colors monochrome and the shapes slim and simple.

Just because your shape has changed, don't
go thinking you can suddenly wear clothes that
didn't suit you before. A bias-cut skirt or dress
has never been Trinny's friend, and it never will
be. When you are pregnant, summer lightness
only works when the print is small or subtle.
Because you are larger, large blossoms make
every mother-to-be look bigger than she needs to.

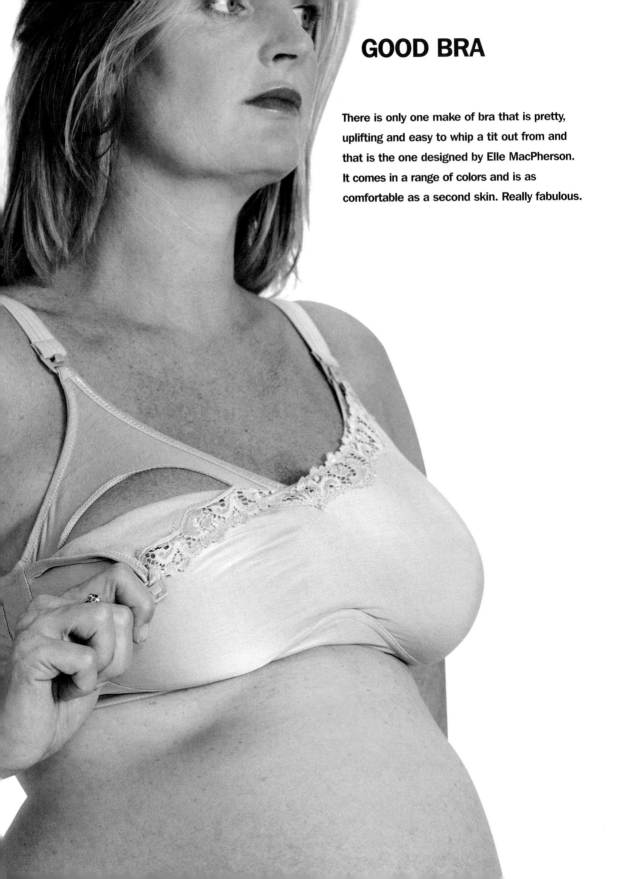

GOOD BRA

There is only one make of bra that is pretty, uplifting and easy to whip a tit out from and that is the one designed by Elle MacPherson. It comes in a range of colors and is as comfortable as a second skin. Really fabulous.

GOOD SUPPORT

When your baby becomes ridiculously heavy, a bit of support for your back and pelvis is a help if you are having to do a lot of standing around.

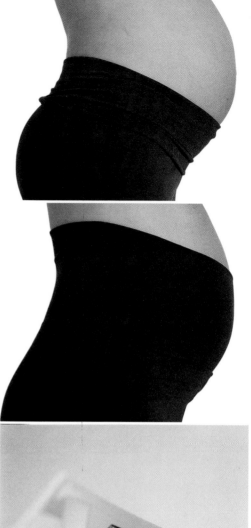

GOOD TROUSERS

We both found these sweatpants (from Christy Turlington's Nuala line by Puma) a lifesaver. The supportive stretch front panel and roll-down waistband can be worn low or up over the bump.

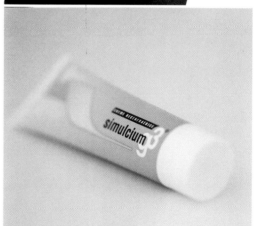

PRODUCTS

If your mother is still around, ask her how her body behaved during pregnancy. If it suffered from stretch marks, water retention, sickness, acne outburst or any other such changes, the chances are you will, too.

Simulcium G3 cream (right) is the answer for anyone in fear of stretch marks. You must be consistent and rub it in nightly.

Micheline Arcier's aromatherapy bath oils, New Breath, are great for softening the skin.

There is no sadder time than the end of breast-feeding for a girl like Trinny. But don't despair, try Sisley's bust cream, called Phytobuste, and the elasticity – if not the generous cup size of your pregnant days – will return.

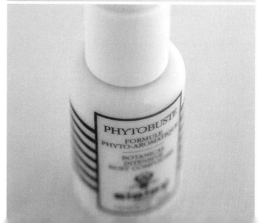

"You don't have to lose your sense of style just because you are pregnant. It's worth making that extra effort for the compliments you will receive."

S

Susan and Jinny Editing

David Design direction

Domenic and Natalie Design

Robin and Aitken Photography

Charlotte Makeup, and Carol too

Christiano & Bev Hair

Mario Color

Jessica Everything...

Zoe & Hayley Styling

Michael Foster Savior

Cat Patience

Caroline Organization

Antonia Dealing with clothing chaos

Oprah For the opportunity

Tracy, Vicky, Lindsay and all at WNTW

Mr. Teoh For safe deliveries

Our husbands For continued support

Jenny and Kelly Bringing up babies

Mrs. Seagrove For Joe and Esme's time off

**and Helle, Theresa, Lynne, Lisa, Kitty, Linda,
Penni, Tracy, Sarah and Mickalina,** for teaching us
so much more about women.